P9-CDF-434

# The Divine Formula

*A book for worshipers, preachers and musicians and all who celebrate the Mysteries*

## Erik Routley

Foreword by Daniel Jenkins

Prestige Publications
Princeton, New Jersey 08540

Cover art work and design by Ruth Robinson

© 1986 Prestige Publications, Inc.
International Copyright Secured. All Rights Reserved.
Printed in the United States of America
Library of Congress Catalog Card Number: 85-63336
ISBN Number: 0-911009-03-5

BOOKSTORE

12 06

16 DEC 86

# Foreword

Prestige Publications is to be congratulated on the initiative which it has taken in making available this previously unpublished work of Erik Routley's, which was found among his papers after his sudden, deeply lamented death. Among his numerous books, none gathers together so richly and in such close inter-relation, his unique combination of concern for preaching, liturgy, history, hymnology and church music. It also vividly expresses his dissatisfaction with anything less than the best in Christian worship, a dissatisfaction which never blunted his pastoral sensitivity to the needs and expectations of ordinary congregations. All it lacks to make it a comprehensive memorial to his characteristic work is some illustrations from the field of detective fiction in which he was also an acknowledged expert.

I am particularly grateful for the amount of evidence which this book provides of his quality as a theologian and as a biblical exegete. To those who knew him as a preacher, this will come as no surprise, but his renown as a hymnologist may have overshadowed this aspect of what he did for us. The freshness of his treatment of some of the parables and the way he writes about the apostle Paul make this clear. His discussion of the Eucharist in relation to the Last Supper may be controversial. No one can deny that it is — what he said good exposition should be —"liberating."

Within the sphere of the arts themselves, his lecturer's paraphrase of Donne's sonnet, "At the round earth's imagined corners, blow," displays his mischievous wit as well as his theological perceptiveness. It also underlines the fact that, as a hymnologist, he knew a great deal about what makes good poetry as well as good music.

American readers will appreciate his discussion of the place of music in their church services and also of public prayer. His views of the former are better known, although it is good to have them stated here again with such good humor and such practical good sense. What he says about the latter, and especially about the widespread practice of corporate prayers of confession, is hardly less valuable. Ministers as well as church musicians will be challenged to think afresh about practices which are, perhaps, too readily taken for granted as customary procedures. At the same time, if they are eager to be "experimental" in worship, they will be prompted to be cautious and self-critical.

The first volume of Hans von Balthazar's massive treatise on theological aesthetics, *The Glory of the Lord,* has only very recently become available in English. It is a great pity that Erik Routley had no opportunity to comment on it in the light of his discussion in his own

iii

74133

book of the relation between the preacher and the artist. He would have found a great deal with which to agree in von Balthazar but we can imagine the delight with which he would have observed that Isaac Watts had said substantially the same, and far more succinctly, in one of his great hymns, "Nature with open volume stands." That hymn was one of Erik Routley's own favorites and I am sure that he would have been content to have it stand as an epigraph for this book.

But in the grace that rescued man
His brightest form of glory shines.
Here, on the cross, 'tis fairest drawn
in precious blood, and crimson lines.

Here his whole name appears complete
Nor wit can guess, nor reason prove
Which of the letters best is writ —
The power, the wisdom or the love.

Daniel Jenkins

iv

# CONTENTS

# I
# *Context*

In earlier books, all now long enough out of print for it to be  1
not indecent for their author to refer to them, I have ventured to
write about matters lying on the frontiers of theology and music.
If my first book, *The Church and Music*, mostly written in 1942-3
and first published in 1950, be regarded as one of these, the period
is now approaching 35 years. In that book I attempted to
approach historically the question of what church authorities had
said about music, and of how attempts, since the early Christian
Platonists, had been made to relate the disciplines of music and
theology. Later, in *Church Music and Theology* (1958), I made
some attempt at a more speculative level to relate the two disciplines. Later still, in *Into a Far Country* (1962), I made an effort
towards formulating a Christian aesthetic, not concentrating on
music. Then, in *Words, Music and the Church* (1968), I approached
the same subject from a more practical angle, trying to handle the
aesthetic of Christian worship.

I am content to believe that this was far from satisfactorily  2
done, but the problem keeps nagging at me. And much more
recently I have been allowed to turn from the professional pursuit
of practical theology (if I may so describe the work of a Christian
pastor, however inadequately done) to the direct pursuit of church
music, and that in a country not my own. I therefore once more
attempt to tackle this elusive subject, and perhaps to present it in a
manner which may be more tractable for Americans than my
earlier essays were. (I must hasten to add that my American
friends were far more hospitable to those earlier essays than were
my own countrymen: indeed so cavalier was the reception they got
at the hands of the learned that my reaction ran out at the other
side of penitence. I could easily have been persuaded that there
was much wrong with them: the end product of what some of these
people said was to make me feel that, to arouse such ire, there
must be something in them).

I suppose that those earlier books were prompted by a vague    3
feeling that something was not as it should be: that the defects of
church music had a theological basis. I think I was struggling
towards the expression of a conviction that the defects of the kind
of theology I cannot bear have an aesthetic basis. To be candid
— and I think that such candor will turn out to be not so much an
exercise in public breast-beating (an activity I admit to be inde-
corous) as part of my initial argument — of those four books, one
was caused by the need to write some sort of a thesis for an Oxford
postgraduate degree, the second by the stimulus of a seminar, the
third and fourth by invitations to lecture on special foundations
which implied the need to produce some new thinking in a field of
my own choice. But this book stands on more solid ground. I wish
first to enumerate certain situations which I have encountered in
(so to express it) both my countries which have obliged me to go
back to this vexatious subject and think it through again, not only
repeating what I said before (though I shall now and again do just
that) but looking in new directions for assistance.

The situation of church music in America is one which posi-    4
tively clamors to heaven for some theological analysis. The cli-
mate of church music is most interestingly different from that
which prevails in Britain, or at least, in England. America is in a
period of intense aesthetic energy. In the limited field of church
music, even the increasingly difficult economics of publishing are
not noticeably discouraging composers from writing, and pub-
lishers from putting out, and presumably music directors from
buying, large quantities of new music. This music ranges from a
shameless mediocrity that makes Barnby sound like Brahms to an
experimental wildness that makes Schoenberg sound like Bach. In
particular the American composers have freely explored the field
of electronic music — not only, as everybody knows, in electronic
reproductions of organ sounds (which now the English do better)
but in the use of tape-recorded sound effects in liturgical music.
The English have not gone far in this direction — for reasons
which in a moment will be obvious. (§8).

Public worship in American churches similarly ranges from    5
the decorously liturgical (for which I fancy one goes now to the
less experimental Episcopal churches) to the fantastically confused (for which you can go either to the post-1964 Catholic
culture or to the more opulent white protestants). In particular,
the way music sprawls over Protestant services in modern America is not a bad introduction to the way music sprawled in the late

European Middle Ages; choral music very often elbows congregational music almost off the stage. Large protestant churches often employ full-time music directors to control anything up to eight different choirs, operate two or three identical services on a Sunday morning, and boast of a music-program which would do credit to an academy of choral music. I can think of one church in the South where the organist is a coast-to-coast celebrity, and where the church plant contains twenty-eight pianos and four full pipe-organs.

With all this opulence, I very rarely meet anybody who asks  6
what its purpose is, or where the massive output of church music and the worshiper's needs actually meet. And I should be the last to express any hope that the musical interest should be extinguished in favor of some pietistic ideal of 'simple worship'. Indeed, I shall insist that except the question be put theologically, and be subjected to the full discipline of reason, it will get answers which will do nothing except discourage a talent which personally I admire and, as an Englishman, envy.

But I can summarize my anxieties at this point by quoting  7
what my friend the theologian Daniel Jenkins once told me. Preaching on Reformation Sunday (October 31st or the nearest Sunday to it) in a Protestant-oriented university chapel where the musical appointments are famous for their excellence, he encountered as one of the anthems Palestrina's *Tu es Petrus*. It is, I know, the custom there to present three choral anthems at the Sunday morning service (which is normally not eucharistic), and to present them with professional competence. But a touch of imagination could be said to have been lacking on that occasion, and there is no reason to think it is present on others.

In contrast, the English church music scene has always been  8
dominated by the cathedral tradition. Historically it is a common error to think that the only English church music worth studying is cathedral music. That error of course is elementary: but it has always been in the beautifying of Matins and (more frequently) Evensong in cathedrals and collegiate churches that English talent has flourished most freely. So English church music is accustomed to a more public style, a greater formality, a greater reticence, and a more conservative environment than it enjoys in America where the Episcopal tradition of anglicanism is a minority culture. If English nonconformist churches were as affluent, as influential and as enterprising as the non-episcopal American churches, a nonconformist 'alternative culture' in church music would probably have emerged in a style comparable to the American. Anthems

with handbells and recorders would have been called for and produced and bought (and we might or might not have been better off). As it is, a non-episcopal culture in England is confined to hymnody (where it flourishes abundantly at present). This is why some electronic experiments I mentioned in passing had no noticeable counterpart in Britain, and why the progress of British church music is perhaps more orderly and disciplined — though not necessarily more creative. But at least in England the place of music in church in the majority culture is better defined than it is in America. The Anglican church, because of the still regulative requirements of Evensong, and the nonconformist churches, simply because of slender resources, are spared the problem of 'music-sprawl' which I venture to detect in America.

In the specific matter of relating the disciplines of church    9
music and theology, I think that, for the very reasons which make music somewhat disorganized in its function, Americans are better placed to pursue research and ask creative questions. In most of America there is much less that is regarded as axiomatic: or perhaps it is better to say that more axioms can be dislodged from their status as axioms and turned into arguing-points. You don't (or in my view you shouldn't) want to get rid of the *Magnificat* from Evensong[1]: you can (or I think you should) ask whether the anthem in a Presbyterian morning service in America is rightly placed and used. But are the questions in fact being asked where people are most free to ask them? On this head I have two points to make, of which this section will deal with one.

A theologian cannot be satisfied with the way in which music    10
is handled in the American seminaries. So far as I have been able to discover[2] the treatment of the subject seems to lie, in any given seminary, somewhere on a line running from furtive philistinism to almost ludicrous extravagance. It was true in 1975 that one very well known seminary presented 78 church music courses from a faculty of 26 instructors, while another equally prestigious institution offered one course for a single semester (that is, half a course) from one visiting professor (whom it would be fair to call half a professor).

I am not so impudent as to attribute any kind of malice,    11
negligence or incompetence to either of these institutions: there is no point in disguising that the second I refer to is that at which I myself worked for one semester in what was one the the happiest periods of my life. But I believe it would be fair to say that you encounter one of two situations wherever you go. Either church music is, as it is with certain southern communions in the United

States, a means of evangelism, and as such a *technique* to be vigorously taught and expertly nourished; or it is a subject which only a few eccentrics will want to know about. It is not in either case a discipline which a theologian need take seriously, or which a pastor will be defectively trained if he misses. It's something, in most places, which you study if you have time and are musical, and which an institution provides if it can afford it. Now I am asking whether there is any other ground we can build on; and I am going to attempt to stake out a claim for a piece of ground to be used for that purpose.

If I am right in such observations as I have been able, or assisted, to make, then I think that the following piece of actual history will contain a clue. The faculty of Union Theological Seminary in New York contained in the nineteen-fifties and sixties perhaps more world-famous names than any other, at any rate in the USA. Reinhold Niebuhr and Paul Tillich, to name only two, were to be encountered there. On the same campus there was a School of Sacred Music, one of the finest of such institutions in the country, again staffed by people who in their field were as eminent as their neighbor theologians. In that block of buildings on the edge of Harlem there was such a concentration of philosophical and musical talent as we shall wait a long time to see again. I have to observe that among all the publications that came out of that campus and travelled all over the theological world, not one, not a single page, appears to have been the consequence of any dialogue between the masters of both disciplines who were living hard by one another. For all the creative interdisciplinary thought that came of it, those faculties might as well not have been on speaking terms. The School of Sacred Music moved in 1971 from New York to Yale University and now occupies part of the premises of the Yale Divinity School. One can still hope for dialogue — but one hardly hopes with confidence yet.

I think nothing quite corresponds to this in Britain, though New College in Edinburgh, the distinguished theological school so close to the University and standing in the true Reformed tradition of philosophical and theological strenuousness, could be a place where one hoped to see something happening. It is significant that the religious pattern of Scotland is so much more like that of America than is that of England, and it is appropriate to observe that New College has had, as long as memory runs, a galaxy of theological talent to draw on.

But I have, for reasons like the above, not been surprised to encounter in such travels as I have been able to make (which one

12

13

14

5

way and another have so far taken me to more than thirty of the States) the constant question, 'How can we arrive at a happier relation between clergy and musicians?' Once again, the question is being asked in America with ten times the energy with which it is being asked in England. Anything from a dinner meeting of the local chapter of the American Guild of Organists to a week-long 30-hour seminar in some academic center like Princeton or Southern Methodist University, Dallas, produces that question. Ask a seminar to propose its own agenda, and within five minutes that is what comes up. I hardly ever encountered it in England — probably because in the majority church it is assumed that the Rector or Vicar is in control of all decisions, and it is no use even raising the question of how his authority is exercised. But in America, where church music is vigorous, where choir-directors and organists are as highly trained professionally as pastors (and nearly as well paid) the question is a live one.

And I am simply not satisfied with an answer which deals    15
merely with administrative details, or stops at saying, 'Well, if the seminaries did their job and the choir colleges did theirs the question wouldn't be there.' I am not satisfied with the assumption that the minister is doing one sort of job and the musician another, and that they simply must treat one another as professionals of equal standing (though if they did that we should have made some advance on many grievous situations that prevail at present).

That is what has prompted the reflections that occupy the    16
following pages. The problem is now, as I see it, both more practical and more tractable than I thought while I lived in Britain. I think I can be less speculative than I used to be, for I find that such modest theological enquiry as I have myself pursued has driven me precisely in the direction that this subject requires. I am going to begin by suggesting that the minister and the musician are both artists and by trying to expose the true nature of the communication in which both are interested. Before I have done I shall, I think, be dealing with issues general and abstract enough to count as theological or even philosophical (but others must judge of that). I shall, however, follow my normal course of writing of theology in terms which I hope are understandable to artists, and of music in terms which I hope will be not unacceptable to Christians who do not claim musical expertise.

But in that commonplace and innocent sounding promise I    17
have stumbled on a point about which I propose to be dogmatic and positive. I am going to refuse to accept the distinctions so constantly made between 'the musical' and 'everybody else' on the

one side, and between 'the theologians' and 'everybody else' on the other. This may be death to any claim I might ever want to make to be taken seriously in either discipline (but it's late now to be troubled about that kind of trifle); I believe I have always refused to accept that pattern, and I now find that for the purposes I have in mind to accept it would be fatal.

There were ages of relative musical innocence — much nearer  18 our own time than any comparable ages of theological innocence — when the distinction between 'the musical' and 'the rest' had no meaning, or no such meaning as it now has. What I find pernicious is the quite normal habit people have of dismissing an argument about music by saying 'ah well: you're musical and I'm not.' I think this is about as plausible a proposition as if somebody said, 'ah well: you're rational and I'm not.' I should agree that some-body might very properly protest in such terms were I to be arguing about the authenticity of the text of the viola part in a Mozart string quartet. But then the protest would mean, 'Look: I'm not interested; you are boring me.' But when, let us say, somebody is arguing for the excellence of the tune which Ameri-cans know to "When I survey the wondrous cross" or of the singing of AMEN after all hymns (against both of which I should myself protest with emphasis), I repudiate his right to retreat from the argument by saying to me, 'ah well: you're musical and I am not' because in arguing about those things at all the other party has admitted that he or she is sufficiently musical to mention them. Almost everybody is musical enough to have opinions, to recognize tunes, and to be misled by the blind guides into bad habits. There is a difference between being tone-deaf and being untechnically musical. In exactly the same way there is a differ-ence between being untheological and being technically untheo-logical. Indeed, even though I can just about conceive the condi-tion of a person who literally cannot distinguish between 'My country, 'tis of thee' and the Dead March in *Saul* — a condition which must be about as unusual as color-blindness — I really cannot conceive that in which a person is totally untheological, for it would probably mean that such a person had no rational faculty at all: if a man can speak at all he can speak about God.

Much mischief is done by our common modern fashion of  19 categorizing and specializing. It is bad enough when the eminent in one discipline cannot communicate with the eminent in another (I am writing this book, as I have said, because of just such a situation between two disciplines between which I want to build at least a telephone line): it is far worse when people assume for their

7

own convenience, to save themselves the trouble of communicating, that the effort is not worth making: when musicians think that only they are musical, or technical theologicans think that only they talk rationally or argue validly about God.

I am in the habit of speaking of church music as music made    20
by, or in the presence of, the unmusical. There I use the word 'unmusical' in its modern sense, meaning that when music is made in church it is made in the presence of, or (in the case of hymns) by people who cannot be assumed to spend any of the rest of their time making music, or making that sort of music. The 'unmusical' are, in that proposition, people whose leisure is not given to music, who do not go to concerts or join choral societies, and are distinguished from people to whom music is, as it were, a native language or a totally acquired language. In the days when Latin was used in the Catholic liturgy nobody thought that every worshiper would be intimately familiar with the *Aeneid* or the Odes of Horace. But it was assumed that every worshiper would have enough Latin to get as much as he wanted intellectually out of the liturgical words. It is the same, I am insisting, with church music.

It is the same, I insist also, with theology, and I am prepared    21
to describe the preacher's activity as the display of theology before the 'untheological'. Indeed when I argue a little later on about the preacher's activity I shall assume exactly that; I shall assume that a listener has enough 'theology' (capacity to talk, or to apprehend argument about God and the things of God) to receive what the preacher communicates. What I am leaving quite out of my argument is the person who has literally and mathematically *no* musical and *no* theological faculty. I am content to believe that virtually no such person exists. I regard it as dangerous and damaging to say that the theologians, or the musicians, are on this side, and the rest on that. The theologians, and the musicians, live in one part of a country which the rest also inhabit; they pursue positively what the rest mostly leave on the periphery of their consciousness. They make an object of close study what to others is just part of the scenery. We may not say that to those others it doesn't exist intelligibly at all.

I am also in the habit of quoting from Book VII of Plato's    22
*Republic* the famous parable of the people in the cave. Plato there says, in the course of his argument about the search for the ideal ruler, that the majority of people must be thought of as imprisoned in a cave, with their backs to its mouth, looking only at the shadows thrown on the inner wall by real objects moving outside the cave behind them, and out of their sight. His 'philosopher

king' is he who goes out into the light, sees the real things, and then comes back to interpet them to the cave-dwellers. Now as a text for an exhortation that parable is just about as dangerous as 'Behold, I stand at the door and knock,' and were it as familiar it would be as frequently misinterpreted. But it does represent the relation between the specialist and the non-specialist in any discipline. It does in some sort represent the function of the church musician or the preacher, who moves about constantly in a world which is his own, among things which mean most to him, constantly exploring further and making more of it his own, and interprets it regularly to people who do not move in it as he does. After this point Plato's parable ceases to be useful, because a musician or preacher knows (and should give full value to the fact) that his hearers or fellow-participants have their own worlds in which they move as freely and expertly as he does in his. They may be doctors who interpret medicine to patients, or carpenters who use their skill to make non-carpenters comfortable, or civil service clerks or computer operators or housewives, all of whom have their world of expertise in which others with and for whom they live are inexpert.

But there is a far more sinister way in which Plato's parable 23 breaks down — or rather is deliberately destroyed. This is when the philosopher-ruler stays out there in the sunshine and doesn't trouble to come back into the cave. This is more and more what is happening in our disproportionately specialized society. There are ministers and musicians who are, in church, cavalier with their congregations and impatient of the non-specialist. The duty and delight of communicating with people who are less specialized and scholarly than one claims to be oneself — of treating them as if they live in the same country and not in a foreign land — is disappearing from the spiritual programs of more and more theologians and musicians (and artists and scientists) as time goes on. I am interested in changing that.

We must never hold our cave-dwellers in contempt. We must, 24 as I said, remember that in other disciplines we are in the cave and they are in the open air. But where the theologian or the musician is the 'philosopher-ruler' one condition of being a cave-dweller must always be allowed for. The cave-dweller can enjoy his shadows very much, but he cannot criticize or analyze them. Their outlines are too indefinite for that. They will make an impression, but that impression will not be censored by any critical faculty as it is in the mind of a cultivated theologian or musician. Now in any area dealing with art — and I am insisting that both these people are artists — this is especially important. For if what I am going to

9

say (and there's nothing new or remarkable about saying it) is true, that the communications of art change people, influence people in a sense in which the giving of information does not, then it is always possible for the shadows to have an evil influence on the watchers. There is no guarantee that because the communication is within the realm of art it is beneficial. There is a pernicious way of preaching, and there is a pernicious kind of music. A trained theologian will at once detect the fallacies, or the unscrupulousness, or the spiritual bullying, in an evil sermon (even if he then decides that he will admit those qualities into his own work for his own purposes: there are plenty of gangsters in this profession); a trained musician will be able to distinguish good music from bad music — even when he argues heatedly with another trained musician about where the boundary runs. But the non-specialist has no equipment for doing that. So what is carelessly or unscrupulously offered to him will go straight into his affections, bypassing the intellect. The toll gate has not been erected: the filter has not been fitted. That is most of the difference between people who live at one end of the country and people who live at the other. This is what Vaughan Williams meant when he made the audacious and now celebrated remark that 'good taste is a moral matter.' 'Good taste' is too weak a word for what we are going to examine: but this is what that pugnacious campaigner was driving at. And he wrote that, not in a treatise on musicology or ecclesiastical art, but in the preface to a hymnal.[3]

I shall then approach this matter by starting out from the assumption that both musician and minister are artists. I worked out in *Words, Music and the Church* the thesis that public worship is an art form. I did not say it ought to be: I said it inevitably and by definition is: and that the only question is whether a particular act is a good or bad example of this art form. Similarly I shall say of the minister that he is (not that he must try to be) an artist, and that the question is only whether he is a good artist or a bad one. I shall speak often of the minister as if preaching — his special art-form — was all he did; having been in that trade myself for upwards of thirty years I do not actually claim that he does nothing else. But primarily he is a communicator, and it is on that ground that he must stand when he is making contact with the musician, who does not usually find it so difficult to think of himself as an artist. But it is time now to attack the first of the philistines' strongholds, and to ask what kind of communication the theologian, in his role as messenger or minister, and the musician, in his similar role in church, are engaged in. And I shall begin on the neutral ground of poetry.

---

[1] Its dramatic force is exposed in *Words, Music and the Church.*

[2] I base this comment on a piece or research done by a team of students at Princeton Theological Seminary in 1975, led by Chaplain James Shannon, who examined and collated the music-programs in 102 American protestant seminaries, taking their data from Seminary Catalogs.

[3] The *English Hymnal*, 1906, 1933, p. ix.

# II

## Poetry, Prose and Preaching

If we begin this journey by taking a brief look at the poet's    26
world, let no reader be discouraged. The object of this excursion is
to set up what we may call the spectrum of communication. For
convenience let us place at one end of the spectrum a poem, and at
the other end the telephone directory, and ask what kind of
communication each aims to effect. It is unlikely that anyone will
doubt that there is a difference.

One consults a telephone directory because it provides    27
instant and complete information on a clearly-defined point. You
expect it to be reliable, and you demand no more of it. Few people
read it as a work of literature. Few people consult it for any
purpose other than the gaining of absolutely specific information
serving an equally specific purpose. As in another context
Sherlock Holmes says of Bradshaw*, 'its vocabulary is nervous
and terse, but limited. The selection of words would hardly lend
itself to the sending of general messages.'

At the other end there is poetry. It is, I suppose, one of the    28
most obvious qualities of such a poem as I am about to quote that
by the use of a very few words, chosen with the skill of a craftsman
who uses them as precision tools, it arouses in the hearer or reader
impressions which could be aroused only, if any other medium
were used, by a very much larger number of words, and which
then, because of the plethora of words, would be confused.

But it is not only that. At one end of our spectrum there is the    29
kind of communication which one may compare with the passing
from hand to hand of an object — a parcel, a book, a piece of
paper, while at the other end there is a communication which is
much more like the throwing of a ball. In the former case, the
recipient simply takes it; in the latter, he catches it — or drops it.

---

*Bradshaw, now lamentably extinct, was a comprehensive English rail-
way guide.

13

In the second, but not in the first, there is an element of risk (he may drop it) and an element of personal effort and satisfaction (if he catches it). In the first case, there is nothing personal in the transaction; in the other, a personal factor which may easily amount to a factor of *change:* something happens to the person who catches the ball.

In *Into a Far Country* I developed this notion, and I am summarizing it here. I there put it in another and parallel way. There are propositions to which the only possible reply is, 'Indeed?' or 'Thank you for the information', said in a normal fairly flat tone. There are others to which there are two possible reactions: either a complete absence of reaction, or an emphatic, excited 'YES!' never unaccompanied by some bodily movement. The spectrum runs between those two experiences. The failure of the 'flat' communication can only be a bored indifference, the reaction one produces when given information one did not ask for, as when one is tediously shown round a city or lectured to by somebody whose communication is in nothing but flat statements. (Compare the way Kenneth Clark showed us all round the universe of history in *Civilization* with the way some people wear you out in conducted tours of what they believe to be 'places of interest.'). The failure of 'dynamic communication' is not boredom but simply plain loss. One difference seems to be that in 'flat' communication the *communicator* (if he is a failure) is quite unaware of any sense of loss, while the receiver is conscious of mounting exasperation; while in the second, if it fails, the receiver knows nothing about it at all while it is the communicator who feels the acute sense of failure. The anticipation of this is what causes artists to live at such high tension.

Or you can simply say that the difference is between what is not precious but only instantly useful — such as the information in the telephone book — and what may be of no practical use but is infinitely precious — such as the content of a poem.

Or again, take the uniquely human activity of conversation. In some company there is talk but no conversation. Perhaps some person hogs the show and drones on and everybody else is bored and frustrated. Or perhaps two people talk antiphonally but without listening to one another. (One is wickedly reminded of Dean Inge's description of the anglican prayer-book response as 'a conversation between two deaf men:' those disjunct and decontexted psalm-verses that precede the Collects do indeed become more mysteriously obscure the more one looks at them). But in some company it is like a good game of tennis; the presence of the other parties makes *you* a better conversationalist than you thought you were, and the experience is refreshing and rejuvenating. The bore is at one end of the spectrum, the good conversationalist at the other.

And good conversation is never without laughter! Laughter can be crude and cruel: it can be embarassing. Plenty of people claim to a sense of humor, but this may merely mean that after making smart remarks they laugh themselves. Wit is what engenders laughter in others, laughter in which there is no cruelty or crudity. I shall not easily forget the memorial service in Edinburgh celebrating the memory of Britain's greatest authority on Alexander Pope, who was Professor John E. Butt (1965). During this service a scholar who was also a first-class reader read a long passage from Pope's *Essay on Man;* now you cannot hear that well read without chuckling with satisfaction as point after point, beautifully and economically turned, goes home. So there was *laughter* at a memorial service for the dead; and it was entirely and felicitously appropriate. Laughter of this sort is precisely what happens when you have 'caught the ball.' There is little wit in the telephone directory: poetry is never without it, even when the poem is as solemn, and the laughter as silent, as is the case with what I am now about to quote. 33

Consider then this poem of John Donne. 34

At the round earth's imagin'd corners, blow
your trumpets, Angells, and arise, arise
from death, you numberless infinities
of soules, and to your scatter'd bodies goe.
All whom the flood did and fire shall o'erthrow,
all whom warre, dearth, age, agues, tyrannies,
despaire, law, chance hath slaine, and you whose eyes
shall behold God, and never taste death's woe.
But let them sleepe, Lord, and mee mourne a space;
for, if above all these, my sinnes abound
'tis late to aske abundance of thy grace
when wee are there; here, on this lowly ground,
teach mee how to repent; for that's as good
as if thou hadst sealed my pardon, with thy blood.

Now let us transcribe this as perhaps it might be presented by a careful scholar who wished to cover the same ground. He will be particularly cautious against any kind of misunderstanding, and against being thought to entertain opinions or superstitions 35 which, if ascribed to him, will damage his reputation. We will suppose him to be addressing an audience on the subject of death and repentance, and, being conscious of his audience's bondage to images, trying to reduce their apprehensions to rational form. His discourse might run something like this:

My subject to-day is repentance, and the necessity of exercising it in this life. Let us suppose that we are destined, after the end of this present mortal existence, to pass into another life. The scriptures of the New Testament, and the creeds of the church, suggest strongly that this is true, and that this is what we may expect. Indeed the First Letter to the Thessalonians, which many believe to have been written by St. Paul, and the fifteenth chapter of the First Letter to Corinth, which we may safely ascribe to him, encourage a belief in a process which Christians tend to describe as 'the resurrection of the body.'

Let us further suppose — and this, of course, is a fantasy —that at some time after death the soul will be summoned out of the grave to a destination commonly described as a heavenly existence. In order to suppose this we must further suppose — which we know to be false — that the earth is flat, not round. If it be not round, then it will be polygonal, and it will therefore have corners. Let us take it (since three false-hoods can do little more damage than one) that it is square, and that at the four corners of that square there stand four angels; we are equally entitled to imagine it a dodecahedron, with an angel at each of twelve corners. No absolute figure is enjoined on us, provided that we imagine an angel at each junction of a side of the figure with its neighbor. We will further suppose that each of these beings has a trumpet, as is suggested in the fantastic and not wholly reliable Book of Revelation, and that the whole choir of angels, four, twelve or however many, blow these trumpets at the same time — probably in unison, and it is to be hoped in tune (for there is no need to add positively disagreeable fantasies to those with which we are already burdened). On hearing the trumpet, we will imagine all these souls emerging from their physical envelopes, their bodies being for the purpose of the picture, preserved intact rather than consumed by fire or decay.

We must now consider by how many routes these bodies, with their immortal contents, found their way into their graves in the first place. I can suggest to you ten such courses which would have brought them there: (1) drowning, (2) fire, (3) death in battle or by some other agency associated with war, (4) hunger, (5) old age, (6) fatal disease, (7) judicial murder, civil war or other instrument of tyranny, (8) suicide, (9) due process of law such as hanging, electrocution or the gas chamber and (10) accident — all of which by the way are mentioned in the above trivial and over-imaginative New Testament source and in respect of which a prudent man can normally provide against their consequences to his heirs by adequate insurance. By any of these routes — I think our list has covered all the possibilities — a man may come to death; and no matter what it was that brought him there, he will be summoned, we are imagining, by the sound of a plurality of brass instruments played by supernatural musicians.

Perhaps we should also make allowance for one other ancient fantasy — namely, that certain persons passed into the so-called heavenly condition without undergoing first the dissolution of death, as in the obscure reference to Enoch (Genesis v) and the clearly imprecise reference to Elijah (II Kings ii) tend to suggest. But allow even for that, and imagine that whatever brought you to death, however tragic, discreditable or inconvenient its cause, you will be summoned to 'heaven.'

It is then necessary to say that your own sin may well be as great as, or greater than, that of any of these at whom you are looking. None of us has any right to imagine otherwise. You may well mourn for those you have personally lost; but while that grief is a personal condition of which none need be ashamed, there is, contrariwise, a personal necessity alongside it which none should overlook. Once the process of death has been gone through, there is no time or opportunity for repentance. Repentance itself is no part of the process which we have, in our imaginations, been contemplating. Repentance is for this world, and it is here and now that you and I can avail ourselves of that mercy which, using again the traditional and to some repellent language of Christian discourse, was offered to us in the death, or as some say, the blood, of Christ.

Whatever else can be said about that paraphrase, the most 36 evident thing is that it is a good deal longer than the original. It is cast in that form in order to illustrate the technique of certain practitioners of what I shall later refer to as the art of preaching who, being in desperate fear of giving rein to their imaginations or of arousing imagination in their hearers, cover themselves at every point against misinterpretation, or against being thought fantastic. Should anybody wish for a different and altogether more respectable parallel, he can refer to the prayer of General Confession in the Book of Common Prayer of 1662 and compare it with that prayer of General Confession which the puritan party sought to substitute for it in their alternative Prayer Book submitted to the Savoy Colloquy of 1661; the familiar prayer contains 132 words, the proposed substitute, 1300 and 172 citations from Scripture in the margin. (See below, §238)

Or take any of those exquisite short poems by George 37 Herbert, such as 'Come, my Way', or 'Love bade me welcome', and attempt to paraphrase it in an explanatory way, and the profane verbiage of the resulting effort will be sufficiently different from the condensed suggestiveness of the original to show this one elementary quality of poetry — its use of few words to communicate great meanings. Moreover — I think perhaps the effusion above suggests a tolerably literate preacher with some sense of the value and rhythm of words. When one adds to this, as one can if one actually does listen to the efforts of many contemporary preachers, the use of blunt tools instead of sharp ones, the use of tools to do work for which they were not designed, the sagging syntax, sideslipping grammar and lubricious logic of so much that passes for Christian utterance, the state of things is far worse. Poetry is, among other things, precise; but it is also a summons to the hearer to stand up and wait for something which he is going to be invited to catch, and the catching of which will afford him high pleasure.

Let us now withdraw and approach this matter from another 38 direction. I am still pursuing the point that a preacher is an artist; and if I have in the end proved that, I shall have also provided all the equipment for arguing, as I have done elsewhere, that worship is an art-form. Let us ask what kind of information a preacher is seeking to impart.

Mere reason insists that a preacher is not a lecturer whose 39 words he hopes a congregation will remember in detail. Were he that, churches would be furnished with desks, paper and pencils, and not even the preaching houses of the vintage puritans were ever so furnished. The behavior of any congregation traditionally accustomed to preaching suggests something quite different. Should any member of it wish to make a note of something memorably said by the preacher he will do so with reverent furtiveness, pretending perhaps to be filling in one of those visitors' cards which American churches so thoughtfully provide.

No: the purpose of preaching is expressed in words very 40 different from those which express the purpose of academic lecturing. The evangelical formula says that it is designed to bring people to decision. With certain modifications which I should myself insist on, this will do very well. I am going later to argue that the preacher makes a capital mistake if he himself presumes to prescribe the decision his hearers are to make. But I am happy with the notion that the preacher calls for something that corresponds to my figure of 'catching the ball'.

My own way of putting it, based on an experience of this craft 41 which claims no distinction but has extended over most of a working lifetime, is that the result one looks for is the decision of some member of the congregation that the difficult letter he or she was postponing writing can now be written; that the quarrel which could not be resolved because of a rigid insistence on his or her own rights can be resolved; that something which he or she felt inadequate to do can now be done. It seems to me romantic and overbearing to assume that everything about every member of a preacher's congregation will at once be changed every time he addresses them. But what one does hope for is that any given person may perhaps go out of church a slightly more complete person, a person more spiritually competent in respect of some specific difficulty, a person in whom the image of God is a shade less blurred, than was the case when that person came in.

It is, as I shall show, immensely important to realize that the 42 preacher does not need to know what the problem is; in most cases he never will know (though now and again somebody may gratefully tell him). The point is that whereas he has been expounding a scriptural text to the best of his ability, the effect on the listener is translated into a situation with which the text may have had nothing to do. I am reminded of the great story of St. John Chrysostom, the great fourth-century preacher in Asia Minor whose sermons remain classics of their kind and always will. The people of his city and his church were in a condition of deep emergency. For some supposed offence against the will of that headstrong though often inspired emperor Theodosius they were in danger of being massacred by his troops. By some means a message got to the Emperor that caused him to stay his hand until their envoy had consulted with him. Tradition has it that the envoy was the aged priest Flavian, who journeyed all the way to Rome and back, and of course whose news of life or death could not be communicated to Chrysostom's congregation until the double journey had been completed. The story is that during the time of profound anxiety Chrysostom, by preaching without deviating at any point from the prescribed lectionary, kept his people calm, dissuaded them from violent action against the troops of the Emperor, and preserved the peace until the news (which in the end was good) was delivered. There is no reason to disbelieve the substance of that. It was not necessary to preach a special series of sermons 'on national emergency'. The message was received and *translated*. The ball was caught; people who could have degenerated into an angry and irrational mob stayed civilized.

That is what we mean when we say that the preacher's object 43 is to change people — or, as I myself prefer to say, to liberate people. And this is done only when the right to take precautions against being misunderstood or unappreciated is firmly renounced. This, I am saying, is what the poet always does — he takes no precautions after his message has been sent on its way. Therefore preacher and poet are brothers.

There are parallels to this process in two major departments 44 of the life of the church which help us towards an assurance that this is where the secret of Christian communication lies. The first of these is in the structure of church history. It was written long ago by G.L. Prestige in that masterly book, *Fathers and Heretics* (1940), than which there still is no better introduction to the thought of the early Christian Fathers, that in Christian speech the word *tradition* has a special and sacred meaning. When a Christian convert of any age, in the early Christian centuries when books were few and unavailable, sought baptism, he naturally passed through a course of instruction. In the most typical case, a young candidate would be instructed in the Faith by an older Christian, no doubt a presbyter; but whatever the age-relation between the two, it was always a case of somebody 'old in the Faith' instructing sombody 'young' in it. The instruction was by word of mouth, and it was known as *traditio*, which is the Latin word for 'handing over'. When the great day came and the candidate was baptized, he was first examined on his Christian convictions and knowledge, and the answer he gave (called the *redditio*, the 'returning' of the instruction, or, so to say, the closing of the circuit) was likely to take the form, 'I believe in God....', from which the classic Christian creeds developed.

Now the word *trado*, from which *traditio* and 'tradition' 45 come, is also the Latin for 'I betray'; it can be used for that kind of 'handing over'. A *traditor* could be he who gave the Faith to a young seeker, or it could mean a traitor. And the secret of which the early church was never negligent was that in fact you could not be certain that even when the *redditio* was made, the circuit really was closed. A candidate who had said 'I believe' might, under persecution, retract. He might never have understood what was said to him or what he was repeating. He might, as the years went on, distort it or misrepresent it or traduce it. And by that time those who might have said, 'Mend your ways: return for more instruction' were dead. The whole communication of the Faith through the generations rested on an enormous risk. It was a risk which death made inescapable. New generations must have the Faith handed over to them. Now the risk is exactly the kind of risk I am interested in enjoining on preachers and in exposing as the artist's secret. For consider first the stupid, weak-willed or unscrupulous Christian who in some way, willingly or not, deforms the Faith he received, and then consider the content of the word 'traditionalism' when it means the over-cautious reliance on a deposit of custom, and at once one sees where the risk can become creative. This is admirably argued in the chapter, 'The Perils of Christian Tradition' in Daniel Jenkin's book, *Tradition and the Spirit\**, and in any case anybody can see how dead tradition can become. The consummation the church hopes for is that each convert shall make the Faith 'his own'; that 'I believe' shall have so real a personal content that the thing deposited in him takes on its own life, ideally becoming flexible and assured in paradoxical — if you like, miraculous — proportions. I may say in passing that I am far from convinced that the modern liturgical substitution of 'We believe' for 'I believe' on liturgical recitations of the Creeds is wise. What I am here speaking of, and am about to take further, is something which in the beginning can happen only to an 'I'.

Secondly, this is surely the secret of the way in which Holy     46
Scripture is expected to communicate with us. Nobody can be unaware of the damage that has been done by people who encourage us to read the Bible exactly as if it were a telephone directory. Such advisers invite us to read it one line at a time, and to expect instant results from the process. Others, who have not been exposed to this blasphemous philistinism but who have not either perfected a technique of reading any sort of literature, explore the Scriptures for themselves and are speedily discouraged by this or

*Faber, 1951

21

that uncontexted horror in the Old Testament, or by this or that monumental obscurity in the translation of St. Paul. In an age when literacy is receding and most people's experience of literature is confined to reading company reports, newspapers or government forms, it is not surprising that the Bible gets into more trouble now than it did when many people read nothing else; for when they read nothing else, they did at least read the whole of the one book they could read, and it is certainly doubtful whether more gross perversions of its teaching were current in days when people read only the Bible than are to be found now, when people read it with what they think is more sophisticated equipment, but what turns out to be exactly the wrong equipment.

The very last thing I should wish is to be taken for one of 47 those who challenge Biblical authority on the ground that the Bible was written by people themselves half-literate — a preposterous proposition in any case; nor would I have any patience with those who assume that in translation much of it is likely to be nonsense. Bible-baiting, denouncing the 137th Psalm and the middle chapters of the Book of Revelation, cutting the patriarchs down to size and drawing attention to the moral defects of Old Testament characters (without reference to the Forgiveness of God) used to be a more popular pastime among the clever clerics than it is now; but even that is not particularly good news. The 'higher-criticism at cut rate' school believed they were guarding Christians against reading Scripture superstitiously: their arguments won't have much influence on people who don't read at all.

But the important thing is the reason why it isn't read at all. 48 Intelligent people now need to be warned against bringing the wrong equipment to the task of reading Scripture. They need, not the kit for reading a report or a scientific article, but the kit for reading poetry: in other words, they need to expect instruction and information less and enjoyment more.

I should even say, knowing that it cannot be a popular 49 opinion, that the recent acceptance by protestant communions of lectionaries, though promoted and encouraged by entirely well-intentioned people, happens to have come at exactly the wrong time. The communions I have in mind are people who are still strangers to liturgical church life. Liturgical life means the offering of life in worship, and liturgical reading is the offering of that reading of the Bible which each person does privately. If nobody does it privately, or if it is done privately but unprofitably, the structure collapses. Lectionaries prescribe very brief passages for reading (and presumably for exposition) in worship. If this is the only time the Bible is opened in the life of the Christian, he will be encouraged in exactly that practice of reading the Bible in short bursts which is fatal to his proper understanding of it. Taking textual fragments and presenting them as detached divine oracles is a superstitious practice, quite out of conformity with Christian intelligence. It is hardly too much to say that it is precisely what Jesus criticized in the Pharisees' handling of the Law. If I firmly disbelieve in taking the Scriptures verse by verse and handing people twenty-word quotations in the hope that these will confirm them in the Faith, I cannot be much more patient with the notion of taking it ten or twelve verses at a time. In plain practice it means nothing whatever to an assembled congregation until the preacher has expounded it.

But this is to place more responsibility on the preacher, and to face him with greater temptations, than his preacher's vocation properly can stand. The less the Scripture speaks for itself, the greater must be his ingenuity. I have not myself, when in pastoral charge of a congregation, been able to resist, at suitable seasons, the compulstion to spread large sections of Scripture (like Genesis 37-50 or the Book of Job) over periods of four or five weeks, giving far larger space to the actual reading of Scripture in the service than is normally allowed, in order to bring people to a consciousness that Scripture is there to be read rather than quoted; and were I to return to that way of life, not all the lectionaries in the world would prevent my doing it again. For the object of reading Scripture in church is to nourish people's love for Scripture, to send them back with renewed zest to their own Bibles, their terms of reference and dogmatic landmarks made more visible by the church's teaching. Just as a sermon is designed to cause an individual worshiper to take up his discipleship again in that state of life to which his Lord (not the preacher) has called him, so public reading of the Bible has to be designed to get him to approach the Bible with a more positive, more interested, and more expectant (because more critical) mind.

Is this to elevate private interpretation above the church's teaching? To my mind, no: but one of the points we shall have to take up in the ensuing chapters is the relation in worship and Christian life between 'We' and 'I'. It will need a steady hand to establish that delicate balance, but we must — a little later — try.

All this, however, is a digression from the main point, which is that if ever a book threw balls to people to catch — including some with, as they say, plenty of top-spin — it is the Bible. If it be regarded as a source of instant information, people will gather

23

from it that they are required by Jesus to hate their parents, that Jesus cursed a fig-tree for not bearing fruit in April, and that the Eucharist is founded in cannibalism. Consequences of the telephone directory approach to Scripture can be as ludicrous as the proposition by an anti-pacifist that his convictions were founded in the Biblical statement 'He maketh wars'. They can also be far more dangerous.

It is surely an advantage that traditionally the text of the 53 Bible has been regarded by the innocent as, corporately, 'beautiful'. The ascription of beauty to it is, I believe, a peculiarly English opinion, based on the strange and memorable rhythms and unusual syntax of the King James Version; these themselves are, through a delicious irony of divine providence, the result of the zeal of the puritan translators to achieve a version as literally faithful as possible to the original, even reproducing word-orders and the uses of conjunctions and particles which were foreign to the English of their own time. In consequence, the version has a beauty the more haunting for being slightly exotic. But — even if this leads in some cases to sentimentality, it was on the whole a great mercy that the King James Version was so memorable and superficially commanding, because when it was treasured, it was also so widely *enjoyed* — a state of things which, again, one would have thought the puritan translators were not much interested in bringing about. By contrast, the flatness and humdrum quality of certain modern translations (I should except the Revised Standard Version of the Old Testament Apocrypha and — a proposition which suggests interesting linguistic notions we must not here pursue — the Apocrypha of the New English Bible) is the product of that cautiousness about not being misunderstood which is the blight of contemporary religious aesthetic. The assistance of beauty is removed from the modern religious seeker.

Take it how you will, the Bible must be approached as a work 54 of art — or an anthology of works of art, though I think that a less useful expression. It communicates its message not by inducing a reaction of 'is that so?' but by generating, after effort and risk, a resounding 'YES!' If Karl Barth said that in every verse of Scripture he saw his own life's story (and if ever there was a "ball throwing" theologian, it was Barth), that is what he must have meant. Until the Bible has evoked an explosively existential 'I', it has not spoken.

If we have established the point that in church history and in 55 the ministry of the Scriptures, the removal of risk is death, we are saying little more than that faith is an essential part of the Christian's equipment. But I wish to avoid language of that kind for a little longer, and to turn now to what seems to be the formula on which all living and dynamic communication seems to work. It will not be too presumptous to call it the divine formula of liberation.

# III

# The Divine Formula

What now follows may remind some readers of the authori-    56
tative statement on the Doctrine of the Trinity in St Augustine's
*De Trinitate;* it will be no more than a pale reflection of the results
he achieved by using the same method. It is also necessary to say
that the late Dorothy L. Sayers, in *The Mind of the Maker* (1941)
— easily her most interesting essay in theology —applied this
pattern of argument to literary criticism, and that my own version
gratefully uses one or two ideas which she there threw out.

Beginning from basic principles and experiences, the For-    57
mula which has its archetypal expression in the Christian Doctrine of the Trinity can be traced in some such fashion as I am
about to show. Concerning the Doctrine of the Trinity itself, I am
myself in no doubt about its timeless sufficiency as an intellectual
formula for our apprehension of the Divine communication.
Three is the smallest plural number (as the Greek language, alone
of those commonly studied in the west, classically admitted in its
three modes of declension — singular, dual and plural.* If human
minds are to grasp the kind of plurality in a single Godhead from
which the dynamic of Faith emerges, then the principle of econ-
omy insists on 'Three Persons'; not more; but also, not fewer.
Patristic studies have made familiar the agonizing debates in the
fourth and fifth centuries of our era which exposed the fierce
hazards of embracing such a belief. But a few examples of the
'Formula' will arouse in any reader's mind a quest for others and,
as I hope, a conviction of its cosmic authenticity.

Have firmly in mind our basic proposition, which is that this    58
is a Formula of the Divine Communication and of Liberation,

---

*In Greek, both nouns and verbs have a 'dual'form as well as singular and
plural. But it was a distinction in logic only: classical Greek virtually
never made use in literature of these forms.

and then consider first the way in which the story of our salvation is set out for us in Scripture.

(1) *The Story of Salvation.* If the story recounted in Scripture  59 is the story of God's ways with his world, that is, of the ultimate and final truths, then it seems to be set out in three main sections — very widely differing in the amount of space required for their unfolding.

In the first place, we are told of Creation in two quite differ-  60 ent figures, one of which is centered in a cosmic joy, the other in a cosmic tragedy. We are told how, so to put it, once communication between God and those best equipped to receive it (people) had broken down, God, as it were, evolved a 'pilot scheme' in which a certain ethnic group was 'chosen' (as one does in schemes designed to be paradigms for more universal projects) to undergo the experiences which all must undergo if they are to find their way back to the main road of communication. We are told of this in terms of individuals and of communities, in literature that ranges from epics like the patriarchal tales to the catalogues in First Chronicles, and later in poetry and prophecy. The literature never strays far from specific human situations and concrete historical events (Psalm 22, say the commentators, is a sick man's nightmare before it becomes a foreseeing of the Passion). We are allowed to see, as history gradually evolves from Abraham to the Maccabees, this people passing through every possible stage of success and disappointment, and its constituent individuals under the pressure of every sort of impossible decision, responding with anything from heroism to bestiality; and all the time the pressure is forwards — there is something (the Messiah is its personification) towards which they are feeling their way. Politics and personalities interfere with the process which God has in his purpose: but the purpose remains, even in the darkest days, undefeated and constant.

Then comes the Incarnation, in which, as Christians by it  61 created are brought to believe, the Word of God was fully spoken, his purpose fully displayed. Just as the whole design was so complicatedly and obstinately misunderstood throughout the ages of the Old Covenant, or the First Dispensation, so it was now misunderstood: and just as everything that was suggested and held before the imaginations of the faithful in the old days is now made fully clear in Christ, so everything that humankind brought to bear to defeat the Divine purpose is now focused in the people's hatred of Christ. And the undefeatedness of the purpose is proclaimed in the Resurrection.

All that is, surely, agreed on by Christians. But notice one    62
thing, which not to notice is to fall into the most serious of all
errors. The story is not complete at the Cross, nor is it complete at
the Resurrection. It cannot possibly be said that either of these
had any transforming influence even on the closest friends of
Jesus at the time they happened. The Cross was ultimate calamity
which only two or three of them even witnessed: the Resurrection
was a miracle of which they could only say. 'How wonderful that
*was!*' when they had come to believe in it. Up to the very moment
when they stood on the hill of the Ascension staring up into the
sky ('Where has he gone now? What do we do?') and indeed for
(what we suppose to be) ten days after that, the disciples, though
wondering and temporarily elated by the Resurrection's contradiction of the Cross, are helpless.

Then Pentecost, only after which the disciples become apos-    63
tles. It is at Pentecost that the group all feel a sense that the Cross
and the Resurrection have a *future,* and that that future is in their
hands and that they can handle it. An immense 'YES!' explodes in
them. More than that — the disciples who admired that miracle-
worker, but were utterly unable to work miracles themselves
(Mark 9: 18), are now spiritually competent. What was, up to that
very moment, 'outside them' is now within them and between
them.

Nothing could be clearer. What was 'outside' is now 'inside.'    64
The communication which had never been more than fitful, and
which the Incarnation *by itself* seemed not to improve but positively to frustrate, has now been established. By what I have just
said I mean to draw attention to the obvious fact that there was
always a far greater apprehension of the divine purpose possible
to the great figures of the Old Testament than there ever was to the
disciples while they were, so to put it, *in statu pupillari.* None of
the Twelve showed, at the time, the slightest sign of rising to the
level of Abraham, or of Moses, or of the second Isaiah, or of the
greater Psalmists. The very glory of the presence of Jesus all but
paralyzed them — and the more the truth of his Messiahship
dawned on them, the more helpless they became.* It was Pentecost that made it possible to form the Church, to write the Gospels
and to declare the ever-present reign of Christ.

---

*Modern liturgical studies and precepts are illuminating the drama of
this story better than the customs prevalent after the Reformation did in
the liturgical churches, especially the Church of England. The Church
Year in the liturgical tradition prescribed four Sundays of Advent,
about 24 Sundays for the 'Gospel' up to Pentecost, and then about 24

(2) *The Pattern of Scripture.* The same thing can be said in a     65
slightly different mode. The traditional threefold pattern of Scripture has logic entirely on its side. Early church customs prescribed
the reading from Old Testament, the Gospels and the Epistles at
the Eucharist. Liturgical custom in England during the unsacre-
mental period placed an emphasis which is now agreed to be
un-historical on 'Morning and Evening Prayer', at which two
readings were called for, one from the Old Testament, the other
from the New. This obscured the distinction between Epistle and
Gospel: but from the point of view of the doctrinal literacy of the
congregation, much was lost when the Eucharist was restored as
the central act of worship, and under the old scheme the Old
Testament was never heard. Here the Epistle and Gospel were
separated in significance but the Old Testament disappeared;
what was more, the substitution of hymns for psalms throughout
the service, when congregational singing was called for, effectively
extinguished the last chances of the Old Testament's ever being
heard. The results of this in inducing a pietistic passivity in early
20th century anglican congregations were far more disastrous
than is usually admitted.

But there is another difficulty. Custom has always ordained     66
that a special priority be given to the Gospel in worship. Anglicans
and Catholics stand when it is read; it is always placed after the
Epistle and therefore carries the dignity that in ecclesiastical circles always goes with a posterior position. Other than anglicans
often feel that whatever else is read, a Gospel passage should not
be omitted. (Such advice was given in a widely read book, *Concerning Worship,* by the Scottish authority W.D. Maxwell, which

---

'after Trinity'. This obscured the drama in two ways, both of which are
on the way to rectification. The first improvement is — or will be if it is
accepted — a much longer 'Advent' period, with emphasis on the Old
Testament: nine Sundays instead of four have been proposed, and those
are by no means too many. Secondly: the return to the practice never
abandoned by Catholics of dating the later part of the Year 'after
Pentecost' instead of 'after Trinity' emphasizes the immense importance
of Pentecost in the Christian story. Pentecost can indeed be a celebration of Christian intellect in the Trinity: but it is not Trinity but Pentecost that historically started everything moving. The Joint Liturgical
Group's suggestion of three Lessons at the Eucharist, one being the
'control' Lesson (O.T. in Advent, Gospel from Christmas to Ascension:
Epistle from Pentecost to the end of the Year) is logical and admirable.
The 'long advent' would give (if we could set Easter at the second
Sunday in April) a ratio something like 9 : 23 : 20 in a normal year;
Easter on the first Sunday of April would make it even better: 9 : 22 : 21.

along with his even better known *Outline of Christian Worship* was a standard textbook in the mid-20th century). But some now question this, and on our present showing, rightly. For while it is hardly disputable that the threefold division of the Biblical literature represents the threefold process of the Salvation Story, it is far from certain that the Gospels should be accorded higher authority than the Epistles, for the simple reason that both are the product of Pentecost. It will not quite do to say that the Gospels have a special authority because they contain the authentic words of Jesus. We can be sure only that they contain what the evangelists tell us he said, and it is always very unwise to build arguments on the simple premise that 'Jesus said' this or that. It is better to say 'Jesus, as Mark reports him, said.' Granted that the memories of the evangelists were sharp and affectionate and that we certainly need not suppose them to have written anything misleading: we may indeed suppose that their memories were far more accurate than those of anybody in our paper-ridden and tape-recorder-dominated twentieth century. But it is manifest that the author of Mark was astray in his interpretation of the incident of the fig tree (Mark 11:20-21); it is probable that none of them quite got hold of the inwardness of the destruction of the Gadarene pigs; and it certainly looks as if something slipped in Mark's account at Mark 2:26 where he credits our Lord with a manifest mistake in saying 'Abiathar' where the Old Testament record insists that the person in question was Ahimelech. We have four Gospel records, with fascinating and illuminating differences of recollection, and because of these differences we could not have managed with fewer. But two things seem to be beyond dispute: one is that the Epistles are as reliable as the Gospels (many of them were written before most of the Gospels) for conveying insight into the mind of Christ, and the other is that, as we have said, no part of the Scriptures is immune from misinterpretation if we will not approach them with the respect that we owe to any supreme work of art.

From this it follows that the threefold division of Scripture is entirely logical, but also that our understanding of any of those parts will be defective if we pay subordinate attention only to any other part. 67

(3) *The Law of God.* | Our third mode of investigation concerns the manner of God's communication as it is apprehended from the Scriptures. Broadly speaking the basic text for the ethos of the Old Testament is Psalm 97:2 'Clouds and thick darkness are round about him: righteousness and justice are the habitation of 68

31

his throne'. The experience of Israel in the time of the Exodus established the form of God's communication. They might not look on him and live (the contradiction of that in Exodus 24, like that at the end of Job, or the aspiration in Ps. 42:2, is regarded as a kind of miraculous exception, and the poets' aspirations are no more than aspirations). But they knew him through the Law. They might not make images of him, but they might write about him and sing about him. So Sinai became central. There, in the Commandments, as they believed, was a summary of what they needed to know about the regulation of the only life they were concerned with. Its Levitical elaborations were sacred in being derived from this revelation. More developed and mystical aproaches to this, such as Psalm 119 or the second part of Psalm 19, show how a sense not only of awe and respect, but also of positive love and affection, built itself up in the choice spirits of Israel: but it was directed to something that had come from God, to God's Word, and it was understood that nobody might come nearer. As for the 'Spirit', it was equally clearly understood that this energy resided only in the distinguished and gifted.

The full unfolding of God's purpose was to be in the future: as yet it was only intimated. With the Incarnation of Christ, the Law of God is re-stated. St. Matthew reports his teaching concerning the new world which he has brought into being in St. Matthew 5-7, commonly called the Sermon on the Mount: this is a summary of what is constantly driven home wherever else in the Gospels we hear of him describing the 'kingdom' or the 'reign' of God. Jesus always insisted that this was not new teaching, so far as Israel was concerned, but that it alone was the right way of interpreting the ancient teaching (Mt. 5:17). What had always been presented as a system of prohibitions and cautions is now presented as an adventure; what had looked repressive, he reveals to be creative when he talks, not about avoiding murder but about avoiding all contempt, and propagating love; not about resenting the slap or the demand to carry a load, but about turning the other cheek and going the second mile.

But so far the real difference between the teaching of Jesus and the teaching of the scribes is that the scribes' rules are perfectly possible and practicable, except where their complexity confounds the simple, whereas the adventures offered by Jesus are, by those standards, quite impossible: especially where their simplicity deceives the clever: you never come to the end of them: you have never 'done your stint': and even the part you think you can do is, to the mind brought up on scribal tidiness, daunting. It has

69

70

32

all gone immeasurably further away once Jesus has transformed it.

Yet we are allowed to pass through all that: from Exodus 20   71 via St. Matthew 5 to I Corinthians 13. And (here is a fine example of the need to read Scripture several pages, not a few verses, at a time), I Corinthians 13 is part of an entirely practical and rather severe letter written by Paul to the most awkward and uncomprehending of all his churches. The chapter before spells out the nature of true community; the chapter following says the first and last words about worship; the chapters before 12 have much to say about matters that are only too mournfully familiar in human perversity. Chapter 13 is the moral key to it all — and the most startling thing about it is its measured understatement. It is poetry, of course — what mighty poetry one can gauge by the futility of all the paraphrases of it that hymn-writers have attempted —but it is poetry precisely because of its urgent simplicity. Take those three passages, from Exodus, Matthew and I Corinthians together and you have the Formula again.

(4) *Revelation.* Or you can put it thus: in the Old Testament   72 there were the 'clouds and darkness' hiding the face of God. In the Gospel, there is his complete self-revelation in the historic Christ. After Pentecost, there is the personal witness of a continuing and inextinguishable body of people. Revelation incomplete gives way to revelation complete — but what is that, until the complete revelation has generated an ongoing witness?

(5) *The moral imperatives.* Again: the moral pressure of the   73 Old Testament (the most enlightened and humane law-structure ever devised) is enshrined in the demand, 'You must'. The teaching and example of Christ engenders in the first disciples a feeling, 'I must try: but I shall not get far.' After Pentecost it is, 'I can!'. This is exactly the significance of Paul's exposition of Christian morality — to be found all over his writings. Romans 7 and 8 take you through the whole story: the impossibility of getting near the perfection that Christ has incarnated, ('O wretched man that I am!') is set straight up against the triumphant cry, 'There is no condemnation!' And Paul shows how it happens: it happens through that gift of the Spirit which takes humanity into God's confidence and makes it possible for his creatures to address him as 'Father'. Formerly 'Outside', then 'Alongside', and finally — 'Inside' — thus the communication has developed to its fullness.

(6) Within *the teaching of Christ* itself, as distilled by St.    74
John, the whole pattern appears in a single verse:
> If you love me, keep my commandments
> and I will pray the Father
> and he will send you the Advocate.    (St. John 14:15)

They must at least do what he tells them (if they can do no better,
they can at least treat him with an 'Old Testament' obedience); he
will do what he alone can do; and the result will be the coming of
the Spirit 'who will lead you into all truth,' and in whose power
they will be liberated to do in the world 'the works that I do, and
greater works than these' (John 14:12).

So much for that. The formula could be found in many more    75
ways, but this should be enough to establish its validity. It is a
movement from the objective that cannot be fully known, through
the objective that can be known, talked to, touched, and crucified,
to the objective that transforms the human 'I'. 'I AM THAT I
SHALL BE' is the archetypal self-revelation of God —in which
the verb 'to be' becomes an active verb and time is (if you look at it
one way) compressed into a moment or (from the other end)
infinitely extended, beckoning believers towards the virtue of
hope. In the Incarnation, the Word of Christ seems to have been
'Before Abraham was, I am' (John 8:58), and the word of everybody else, 'What manner of man is this, that the winds and the
waves obey him?'. After Pentecost, the invitation is to an existence
described as 'Not I, but Christ in me'. Thus is established continuity, the overlap between the three dispensations: God in Christ
— Christ in me. For the Old Covenant, 'I AM' is sufficient: the
Name that cannot be named and must be written with consonants
but no vowels. For the Incarnation, the destroyed Perfection. For
the Spirit-filled believer, the superlatively positive 'YES!' From
this our argument proceeds in two directions, and we will first
follow the formula as it illuminates human communication.

# IV

# *Processes*

Turning now to human communication, we must consider    76
the work of the artist. We had better recall that our first two
chapters threw up certain ideas which the third chapter was not
immediately concerned with: notably, the proposition that the
dynamic form of communication has a kind of trajectory like that
of a thrown ball, and the associated notion that in all dynamic
communication there is an element of risk.

How then does this sort of communication — the good    77
conversation that produces wholly kindly laughter and that generates growth in its participants — work itself through?

There is in the first place the impulse to communicate, which    78
becomes, in the artist, urgent enough to be called a duty, or
anyhow an imperative. The artist has his material lying before him
and his medium to work in. In this he is above the angels but lower
than God, who in his primal act of creation created the medium
and the material. But observe how the first Genesis story of
creation opens. It leaves the reader with two utterly contradictory
ideas which none the less it harmonizes as it unfolds. On the one
hand, creation is a timeless explosion of energy: on the other, a
laborious and logical working out of the plan. It begins, 'Let there
be light!' and then takes us through the six-storied structure, in a
single page doing all that a human mind can do to communicate
the mystery of the beginnings of things. It is itself only a beginning, but in that beginning we already see a long way. The explosion, as it were, is God's single and personal act. The working out
is expressed with such prescience in Proverbs 8:22-31 —

    When he established the heavens, I was there,
        when he drew a circle on the face of the deep,
        when he made firm the skies above . . .
        then I was beside him, like a mighty workman.
Already there is an Other: God is moving towards his world, and
at the same time away from it. There is a new Process, a new

Being, which the author of Proverbs personalizes in his poem, and whom St. John celebrates in his Prologue: 'the same was in the beginning with God. Without him was not anything made that was made.' The principle of explosion is at once followed by the principle of order, of becoming intelligible, palpable: that Principle turns out, in the fulness of time, to be Christ, through whom, as theology says, all things came into being and to whom all things tend. In our beginning was, indeed, our ending. 'Before Abraham was, I am.' In Christ mankind is brought back to the archetypal plan, not thrust away from it. It was all there from the beginning.

Thus theology, wrestling with the indescribable. And there on the other hand is Mozart. It is often said of him (because he once said it of himself) that he could see, or hear, a whole opera which he was about to compose, in a timeless moment. Even if the story is apocryphal it is true. 'This is what it will be' is an essential moment in the creative process. In an intermomentary flash a whole creation can, in a sense, unroll before the creator. Then at once — the spadework and the sweat: the work of so organizing a creation that it will travel: its spreading out into time. The timeless thing must be 'incarnated' so that people can touch it, handle it, hear it, and say 'That which we have seen and heard we proclaim to you.' Mozart puts pen to paper and writes. And he or any creator will tell you two things: first, that in the long-drawn-out process of making the creation intelligible there is indeed sweat and wrestling; and second, that as this goes on, subsidiary 'explosions' light up the journey, generated in the actual course of composition — the detail here or there that the painter never foresaw in his initial vision: the inspired little passage that turns some routine moment of musical form into a transfiguring experience (the 'return bar' at the end of the exposition of the *Hammerklavier* of Beethoven, the return to the recapitulation in the slow movement of Mozart's D major String Quintet: perhaps that famous 'wrong turning' in the recapitulation of Beethoven's Eighth Symphony, first movement, or the similar one in Schumann's Piano Concerto). — Man is not like God, and God's thoughts are not as his: but if ever he comes near to that apotheosis which such thinkers as Irenaeus predicated of him, it is in these moments when, as a creator, he listens for the 'explosions' in his nascent creation. Too much control, and these will never happen, and it will be pleasant but routine: too little, and the pressure that builds up to prepare the way for them will never build up. The more difficult he finds it to resist the temptation to stand in the way of his creation's autonomous development, the less likely he is to produce what others will rightly delight in. If God produces a creation which in its turn can produce an Isaiah, a Paul or a Beethoven (and can produce an Al Capone or a Hitler), his child, the human being, can produce not only the grandeur, but also those self-generating details, of a creation in the world of art. It is not a matter to be measured in days, hours and minutes, but any artist knows what an expression like 'the fullness of time' in the Scripture means, just as he knows what it means to say that the creation 'groans and travails'.

Thus far, Mozart has finished his manuscript and sent it to 80 the printer. Being Mozart, he has written one more perfectly proportioned and perfectly communicative piece, whether it is an opera or a minuet. He did this by 'standing aside' when it was right to do so, releasing creative energy when it was right to do so. But when the thing is published, and given its first performance, what happens? It has been sent off on its travels: the composer has given it wings and an engine. But he has not gone with it. Everything now turns on whether those who hear it receive what it is carrying. Everything turns on whether they catch the ball, or if you prefer so to say it, a few of the thousand balls projected by the composition. And an artist can be as surly as he likes in his assertions that he could not care less what people think of his work: but in the end he knows he has failed if they do not catch that ball. And he knows that he must not lift a finger to help them catch it. He must not lower its trajectory. He cannot recall it. He must not attempt to explain it, justify it, defend it. It has gone, wholly gone. The poem is in the book, the symphony is on the program, the picture is on the wall, the cathedral is built, the play has had its first night.

Scripture insists that this process at any rate reflects exactly 81 the relation in which the world's Creator has always stood to his Creation. How often Jesus unfolded the mysteries of his Kingdom under the figure of an *absence:* the master of the vineyard who went on a journey; the employer of the so variously talented servants who went to a far country; himself, asleep in the storm; the remote and inattentive judge; the humorous employer whose lofty justice paid the same wage for one hour's work as for eleven. His mind was quite clear on the question of how much we could expect God to interfere with his creation. All this is teaching about, so to say, the second of the three processes. It is the starting point for the answers to such diverse questions as 'Why does not God remove suffering and evil from the world?' and 'Would it have been better if we had a photograph of Jesus?' Mankind is required to manage the vineyard, to steward the talents, to keep the boat afloat, to worry out the problems of justice and economics without divine promptings. The divine assumption is that all the evidence he needs is there and always has been (which is the argument of the second half of Romans 1).

The Evidence is what the theologians and the Scriptures   82
mean by the Word of God — all the expressions of his divine nature that have been given to us, right through to Jesus Christ himself. 'I see that all things come to an end: but thy commandment is exceeding broad.'; 'the law of the Lord is perfect, refreshing the soul. . . the commandment of the Lord is pure, enlightening the eyes.'. . . and what that law and commandment is it is the proper business of doctors, scientists, economists and politicians to interpret.

Now before we move into the Third Process, let us consider   83
how this applies to a much more elusive art form — the art of preaching, and that of liturgy. Here we will borrow an admirable expression from Dorothy L. Sayers, coined in *The Mind of the Maker*, and consider what happens in human affairs when we encounter a 'scalene Trinity' — a disorder in one of the processes. At this point it will be one of two lines, not of three, that is out of drawing, but what will be very evident at once is that when human beings seek to share the divine activity of creation (which the divine grace invites them to do) things can go wrong.

Dorothy L. Sayers adequately illustrated from literature the   84
results of failure in the three processes of communication, and any who can find a copy of her book should consult it. We will here consider the preacher in whom there is no 'explosion'. He will, of course, be one kind of dull preacher. What he has to say will be second-hand, dug out of books perhaps, or desperately thrown together out of clichés his background and training have furnished, but it will not travel because it has no explosive power behind it; it will drip limply from the pulpit and fall dead on the floor, because it is not in any sense *his*.

Once I was called on to advise a young preacher who was   85
boring his congregation to distraction, and, not knowing what else to say, said to him, 'Is there anything you are angry about?' It was, I now see, dangerous advice because it was partial. It might have had the effect of substituting for learned and indigestible addresses pompous political speeches of a drearily egotistical sort. As we said back in §79, it is not only an initial inspiration that is needed, but an incommunicable quality of being able to control, and yet to leave free, that which one is creating: of allowing the

explosions which the creature generates to supplement, illuminate, and make communicable the initial explosion which the 'idea' supplied. It won't travel without being initially sent off from the shore to the launching pad, but it must have within it its own principle of combustion. To be honest, I don't really know in what terms I could have given that advice, even if I had had the wit to see its necessity.

That is a trivial illustration, and obviously mere indignation is not a good propellant for the Gospel. But if we are analyzing the causes of failure in communication, the cause will always in the end be found to be lack of fuel and lack of spark. I hasten to add that I am not unaware of the devil's conspiracy, ably supported by human agencies, for pouring cold water into the tank. Before we have done we shall be quite clear about the need in any folk-artist of the kind that preachers are to have some assurance that people expect something of him and want what he is offering. In my own view the decline of the art of preaching, like that of lecturing, has gone quite far enough. Those who seek to deflate the egos of preachers and academics have done their work very well and can now stop. We need no more manifestos proving that sermons are out of date and should be replaced by discussions, or that lecturing in an academic context is an unsufferable imposition and should be replaced by a friendly chat. That protest against protest is needed more in England than either in Scotland or in America, and it should be transmitted without shame or hesitation. But when we have said all that, we know very well that the lecturer who is still reading the manuscript he prepared thirty years ago, and got from the books of others even then, will dissuade all but the hardiest spirits from the discipline he professes to serve, and the preacher who copies out the commentary and thinks he has provided food for his congregation will very properly empty his church of all who are not supernaturally loyal or deaf. <sub>86</sub>

Failure of organization, however, is an equally clamorous temptation. And this can take two forms: too much interference with the material or too little. The legitimate interference is confined to the 'ordering' of the material: the 'setting of bounds that it shall not pass'; in this particular branch of art, one of the disciplines is the actual fitting in of the composition to a conventional time slot, and the practitioner has to try to achieve the ability to speak for four minutes without being trivial or for forty without being boring, and to know the difference between the occasions that call for brevity and those that call for expansiveness — as <sub>87</sub>

Beethoven could be equally eloquent in his Ninth Symphony (op. 125) or one of his pianoforte Bagatelles (op. 126). But one of the secrets which are known both to the preacher and to any other kind of artist is how to resist the temptation to turgid complexity, to the crowding of the score or the canvas, and (as I ventured to say many years ago in *Church Music and Theology*) one of the healthiest texts to have in mind is that passage in Leviticus 19 where the harvester is forbidden to go twice over his land with his reaper, but commanded, if anything has been left on the ground, to leave it there for the orphan and the wanderer. The temptation is to pack too much in, born of the fear of being thought insufficiently learned, or in fear of being outrun by the minds of the alert in the congregation. Knowing what to leave out, what to discard, what to leave for later treatment, is a most necessary part of a preacher's skill. Simple laziness, however, can reduce intelligibility. There is more in the art of organization than the rule-of-thumb 'three point pattern' so beloved of homiletics professors, but it is possible for the preacher to become so interested himself in his subject as to make it incomprehensible to his hearers.

But by now it is becoming increasingly clear that we cannot    88
go much further than this until we have encountered the third process — the process, we said, over which the artist has no personal control beyond that which he exercises in the second. It is what happens when the message has travelled and reached the listener. A preacher sends it off on its travels and it falls to earth —in as many pieces as there are people listening. What he hopes to achieve, in his capacity as an artist, is what we said in chapter 2 (§43), which can be expressed in the single word, liberation.* This is what all liturgy hopes to achieve, and it corresponds exactly with what was done for the apostles at Pentecost. Just as Jesus, as recorded in John 16:7, assured his friends that 'It is good for you that I go away,' so the preacher's work is not done until he has assured his people that it is not to him, but to the Father, that they must look for their guidance: and that *now* they can relinquish their dependence on him, and communicate without his help with the Father. This is a state of things, which, human nature being what it is, does not endure for ever, and does not achieve completeness, probably, in a lifetime. It may be only for a day or two that any person is in touch with this 'pentecostal'† experience;

---

*Although I am conscious that at present this is a theologically loaded word, my own definition of it will become clear, I hope.
† Another loaded word whose burden I wish to remove.

only for an hour or two. But (a) once a person has been visited by it he becomes more vulnerable to later attacks, and (b) the need for repetition is exactly what the regular practice of liturgy is there to provide. It is why preachers always, to some extent, 'preach to the converted' (see §162).

The analogy with art of other kinds is much easier to see in 89 this process than in the others. The corruption of this process can again take two forms, which spring from either too little, or too much, interest on the artist's part in getting the required 'YES!' reaction from his hearers. Too little interest in this result (which, we say again, can be controlled only in the second process, not at all in the third) can produce what people helplessly admit to be excellent but indigestible material. For any artist to be over-cavalier about the achievement of the 'YES!' is a peevish affectation. It is his duty, precisely, to *want* it very much and then to renounce his right to control it, not to lift a finger to get it, once the second process has been gone through.

But equally pernicious results, indeed often more pernicious 90 because more delusive, come from an excessive desire in the artist to please. Probably church music provides the richest field for the exploration of this corruption. It used to be said that if you want to study irrational and sentimental music, you must go to that of the nineteenth century. It is now only too clear that the twentieth is very little better. In the English Victorian era there was a great temptation before the composers — cheerfully assented to by many — to please a complacent bourgeoisie whom they (with notable imprecision) believed to be in control of the churches. In the twentieth century other cultures have put in their claim to be pleased — the young, the rebellious, the followers of what has been called the 'pop' culture; and the music designed to gain their approval has a record no better than that of the abused Victorians. It is, we hasten to say, not invariably so. To compare the musical contents of popular hymnals produced in Germany such as *Christen Lieder Heute* and *Schalom* (both 1971) with those of, say, the English *Youth Praise* (1966) is to see two very different approaches to the demands of radical youth; and to compare the literary quality of 'O God of earth and altar' with that of 'They'll know we are Christians by our love' is similarly to see two very different approaches to social anger.

But in the wider field, it hardly needs saying here that the 91 temptation to please, when it is a temptation to control the reaction of the receiver of the message, is a corrupting influence because it is an intrusion of the work of the Holy Spirit.

41

What are we to say, then, about some of the distinguished    92
composers of the past who please us more than they pleased their
contemporaries? Of J.S. Bach, who was allowed to remain in local
obscurity for two generations after his own death; of Schubert, so
much of whose work was neglected in his lifetime; of Beethoven,
who so constantly alarmed his contemporaries with new and
strange sounds? The answer would be simply that the failure or
success of the threefold process does not have to be judged in its
author's lifetime. Mortal men and women take the risk of communication, which, like the risk taken by the early church (§44-45)
is very largely shaped by the fact of their mortality. It is not
particularly helpful to insist that Mozart and Beethoven and
company are people, who don't need to worry about that because
they are 'great'. To *know* that one is 'great', that is, accepted and
listened to by one's most perceptive fellows, is instantly fatal to
any artistic enterprise (or any other kind). That has nothing to do
with it. What history affirms is that because of their poised skill in
operating the second process these people were right in being
unconcerned at what point in history the messages came through.

Correspondingly, it is unwise of any person, or any particular    93
generation, to claim to be wholly sure and irrevocably persuaded
that this or that artist has failed to communicate. True, it still
looks to most of us as if William Blake, in his longer and later
works, communicated less freely and universally than, say,
Wordsworth; it still looks as if the organizing process was not
adequate in his case to the immense volley of explosions that
preceded it. But even there we should never be sure. People at one
time were very sure that Beethoven's last String Quartets and his
*Mass in D* failed to communicate; an orchestra rehearsing the first
performance of Schubert's C major Symphony (the last and greatest) is said to have broken down with laughter at the repetitions in
the string parts of the final movement. Perhaps musicians are
especially impatient and more likely to be wrong than others in
such matters. And of course our present age has seen so many
missiles thrown at us by artists specializing in various forms of
top-spin that the impatience of those who feel defrauded of communication has in some places built up even into political censure.

But somebody will at once want to bring in evidence of the    94
case of J.S. Bach, who, as is well known, was really hardly heard
of as a composer outside his immediate circle during his lifetime,
and whose standing among the great and popular had to wait
really for the twentieth century. (His music was first heard in

42

public in England owing to the influence of Mendelssohn and Samuel Wesley in the second quarter of the nineteenth century — but even then for a long time he was the property of specialists). This, however, is a special and, for our purposes, an unusually interesting case. Any eighteenth century musician expected to work more or less 'to order' — Mozart is supposed to be the first who challenged this way of life, and who accepted the consequent economic insecurity. Bach was typical of that way of life. In secular employment he wrote secular music: in church employment (at Leipzig) he wrote church music. He wrote because he was paid to write, and whatever romantic fantasies people may entertain about the corrupting influence of that way of life on an artist will collapse at the sight of Bach, or of Haydn.

Haydn, however, became a 'great composer' well before 95 Bach. (Lowell Mason, the liberator of American music-making in the 1820s and 30s, founded a Boston Handel and Haydn Society, not a Boston Bach Society). Dozens of secondary eighteenth century composers, now well known, carried on their professions in the same way, turning out admirable, though not necessarily epoch-making, music with efficient regularity and, as in the case of Telemann, piling up enormous stores of graceful stuff which modern scholars have unearthed. Bach in his Brandenburgs and Suites, Haydn in his symphonies and divertimenti, and the rest in their concertos and occasional pieces, wrote to amuse: they wrote often what the great houses of the 18th century used for 'muzak'. Later ages approach their music with an attention which it deserves but which when it was first heard it rarely, if ever, received.

Now this makes them what we are obliged to call 'folk artists', 96 purveyors of what most people in their time regarded as disposable music. The distance their music travelled and the speed of travel depended on what kind of 'folk' they were ministering to. Large and influential houses gave it a good start. St. Thomas Church at Leipzig, itself disapproving and philistine about Bach's work, made a much less satisfactory publicity-source. For this accidental reason, in 1800 Haydn (and for parallel reasons Handel) would be regarded as communicating far better than J.S. Bach. (The name 'Bach' at that date would have been more likely to mean one of Bach's descendants or collaterals than J.S. himself). This is the difference between what we call a folk-artist and what we now think of as an artist *simpliciter*. Nowadays an artist to us is one who paints his picture, and there it is on the wall: who writes his symphony, and there it is in the concert program. It is

43

still difficult to think of somebody who writes a cantata every week or a divertimento every couple of days as an artist on the grand scale. Nine symphonies command our respect more than a hundred and four — Beethoven has a higher throne than Haydn. But this is all nonsense. If Bach wrote his profoundest music to be played on the organ as a commentary on the well-known hymns of his day, the way any tenth rate organist to-day might produce an improvization on CRIMOND, that does not say anything about his qualities as an artist. Only recently have people come to see how profound the Eighteen Chorale Preludes or the larger works in the *Klavierübung* Part III are.

All this would be no more than an irrevelant digression were it not for the fact that the Christian preacher is in exactly the same sense an artist and a folk-artist. He cannot be content with nine sermons and twenty week-night addresses. But the fact that he produces his work 'to order' and with efficient regularity does not in any sense make him a less significant artist than the poet whose life-work is to be found in a slim volume. Not for the preacher the once-for-all composition which is there on the wall, or which is there often in the program, or which is there built to last through the ages. His sermons may be literature fit to print in a book, but that is almost accidental. His utterances may be, like Isaiah's and Jeremiah's, even more significant to later ages than they are to his own (as Bach's have been). But he remains an artist, concerned to communicate to people he can see, unconcerned about the effect, or the enduring quality, of what he says beyond the edification of the 'folk' he lives with. But if in adducing Bach and Haydn we have made some gesture towards the dissipation of romantic clouds from our understanding of the artist's work, we must at once say that the purpose of this was to leave the way clear for us to approach a far greater mystery. To that we are about to turn.

97

44

# V
# Death and Liberation

The mystery for which we have not yet allowed in discussing     98
this Formula can be expressed by saying that the Formula is of 'no
human shape:' or that, once the Formula takes flesh, a dark event
takes place. The Formula says that the divine purpose moves from
the creative explosion through the redemptive toil to a new explosion — "YES!' — in which the receiver of the Word grows, is
changed, moves a step forward along the road theologically called
sanctification (II Cor. 3:18). But St. John wrote: 'He was in the
world, and the world was made by him, and the world knew him
not.' That expresses, as it were, processes 2, 1 and 3 in that order:
but process 3 is preceded by trouble. The New Testament story
places the crucifixion between the work of Christ and its results in
human beings. It was necessary, not only that he should go away
(John 16:7) but that he should be made away with. Athanasius, in
that unforgettable argument in *De Incarnatione,* spells it all out.
'Why must Christ die?' — the question is written down there again
and again: 'Why must he die *like that?*' The answer was that
anyone must die in the ordinary course of things and that therefore the perfect Man, for whom death cannot even to the superstitious look like a penalty for being mortal, must die voluntarily,
and the perfectly good Man must die publicly, and the perfectly
innocent Man must die in disgrace. Only such a death, says
Athanasius, could achieve the results that lay in the purpose of
God from the beginning, to which plan Jesus was unswervingly
obedient.

Nobody knew better than Athanasius that the reduction of     99
the mysteries of the Passion to cold reason is profane. There is
much for theologians to note and use as a warning in the passionate protests of Kierkegaard and William Blake. Here is Kierkegaard in 1849:

It is the tolerance of the orthodox which best shows how
completely Christianity is lost. Their solution is: if only we

45

may keep our faith to ourselves the world can take care of itself. Merciful God! That is supposed to be Christianity! *That* is the power which once broke upon the world and through readiness to suffer forced Christianity on the world, compelled it more forcefully than any tyrant.

The orthodox do not suspect that this, their tolerance, is the effect of sheer worldliness. . . . What makes the position more terrible is that this 'tolerance' is willing to allow the tremendous falsehood to continue, namely for the whole world to call itself Christian, when the private belief of the orthodox is nevertheless that the world is pagan.

How low has Christianity sunk! How powerless and miserable has it become! It is reason that has conquered: reason that has tyrannized enthusiasm and the like, making it ridiculous. This is why people dare not be enthusiastic, do not acknowledge that martyrdom is a glory beyond all comparison; they are afraid of being laughed at instead of being put to death — and so people come to an agreement; they wrap themselves up in their donkey-skin only asking to be Christians themselves, call that tolerance, and flatter themselves that they are true Christians.*

Christianity without a 'YES!' — religion to provide private comfort for the literate — that is what debased reason can bring us to, and what our Formula would bring us to if it did not make room for a martyrdom and a death in every one who wishes to communicate. The same thought was in the mind of Blake, surely, when he wrote the paragraph that precedes the poem so may of us know as 'Jerusalem', and our frequent use of which as a patriotic song is a beautiful example of a nation's catching a ball which a poet never intended to throw:

The Stolen and Perverted Writings of Homer and Ovid, of Plato & Cicero, which all men ought to contemn, are set up by artifice against the Sublime of the Bible; but when the New Age is at leisure to Pronounce, all will be set right, & those grand Works of the more ancient & consciously & professedly Inspired Men will hold their proper rank, & the Daughters of Memory shall become the Daughters of Inspiration. Shakespeare & Milton were both curb'd by the general malady & infection from the silly Greek & Latin slaves of the Sword.

---

*Kierkegaard, *Journals*, tr. Alexander Dru, Fontana Books, pp 173-4.

Rouze up, O Young Men of the New Age! set your
foreheads against the ignorant Hirelings! For we have Hirelings in the Camp, the Court & the University, who would if
they could, for ever depress Mental and prolong Corporeal
War. Painters! on you I call. Sculptors! Architects! Suffer
not the fashionable fools to depress your powers by the prices
they pretend to give for contemptible works; believe Christ
and his Apostles that there is a Class of Men whose whole
delight is in Destroying. We do not want either Greek or
Roman Models if we are but just and true to our own Imaginations, those worlds of eternity in which we shall live for
ever in Jesus OUR LORD.*

Those two monumentally exaggerated protests from the 100
romantic age against the tyranny of reason — represented for
Blake in those humanist classics which were so much exalted by
the atheists of the French Revolution — need have no effect on
any Christian's respect for that divine Reason which they call the
Word of God. But if a Christianity that has no whole-hearted
affirmation at its center is, as they say, no faith but only a pastime,
then no Formula we can claim to extract from it can possibly be
anything but delusive unless somewhere it has death in it.

The Cross of Christ can, in the wrong hands, become an 101
object of sentimental, irrational, uncommunicative adoration; it
can be used to induce in believers sentimental despair and elabo-
rate, sterile quietism. Even martyrdom — which properly is the
placing of a purpose higher than the value of one's own life and
implies the Communion of Saints through whom after one's
personal annihilation the purpose will be achieved — can be
corrupted. It is immortally celebrated in Hebrews 11; in north
Africa in the time of Cyprian (250 AD and onwards to 258) it
provided one of the ugliest pages in all church history. But death
and martyrdom are things about which the artist knows. He
knows them in the sense exactly of Hebrews 11:39 - 12:2:

> They did not enter upon the promised inheritance, because,
> with us in mind, God had made a better plan, that only in
> company with us should they reach their perfection....
> With all these witnesses to faith around us like a cloud, we
> must throw off every encumbrance, every sin to which we
> cling, and run with resolutions the race for which we are
> entered, our eyes fixed on Jesus, on whom faith depends from
> start to finish: Jesus, who, for the sake of the joy that lay

*W. Blake, Preface to *MILTON* (1804-8)

ahead of him, endured the cross, making light of its disgrace, and has taken his seat at the right hand of the throne of God. (N.E.B.)

The notion of the Communion of Saints is followed up in our 102 final chapter §§ 346 ff); for the moment the point we want to emphasize is the renunciation on the part of the individual artist of control of the effects of the Third Process. It is in the Second, and there alone, that the artist takes his decisions and makes his plans. The only way by which he can do this is to be ready to extinguish the self, the 'I', which the 'explosion' brought to life. Nothing less will make communication an agent of liberation. Without this death there can be no raising up and glorifying of the 'I' in the receiver of the message.

So we must go further into a description, in as far as it can be 103 attempted at all, of what happens to the receiver of the message. What is this 'I' that the artist calls into being and nourishes, and for which he gives up his own 'I'? If we can expose this, we shall see what is the purpose of the martyrdom.

I have already called this liberation, and liberation is what I 104 mean. Beginning from the further end, I would call in evidence a recent book by Daniel Jenkins, *Christian Maturity and the Theology of Success\**, a book brief enough to be read at what even this impatient generation would allow to be a short sitting, but profound enough to change a whole generation's way of thinking. It describes the qualities of maturity which the Christian Gospel is supposed to foster, and in a moving passage near the beginning (chapter 2) it shows how the qualities enumerated in the Beatitudes are qualities into which the Christian grows, not qualities achieved only by the renunciation of growth. The book is also an attack, the more damaging for the gentle and generous terms in which it is expressed, against that theology of failure, that caricature of the complacency Kierkegaard complained of in the passage quoted above, which is in fact so fashionable in to-day's church.

The point to establish first is that the life of the Christian is a 105 growth, a pilgrimage, an irregular but (at any rate in God's plan) a persevering progress towards what St. Paul calls 'the fullness of the stature of Christ'. All images of the spiritual life in the Christian tradition have used the figure of movement: the story of the Exodus is constantly referred to as a paradigm of the journey from bondage to freedom, from Egypt to the Promised Land.

---

\*S.C.M. Press, 1976

But the Christian tradition also speaks of a turning point, a 106
new beginning, in St. John's words, a new birth, which corresponds to our 'explosion' just as the process of sanctification corresponds to the 'ordering'. And in fact the process, as it works itself out in time, is not so much like the steady growth of a plant as the progress of an internal combustion engine — a series of 'explosions', as it were, of which the initial one is naturally regarded as especially important, but which get us nowhere if the initial one is the only one (§79). Countless times in a lifetime, as we repeatedly say, a person is galvanized into growth by an experience that produces the 'YES!' Just as creation has a beginning and also a working out, and yet these two are not really to be thought of as wholly distinct in time ('a thousand years are as yesterday, and one day as a thousand years'), so both in artistic creation and in the Christian life, explosions punctuate the 'ordering' process. But each 'explosion' is a moment of change; and the constituent factor in that change is a liberation through death. Liberation of what? Death of whom? The formula here, always and inevitably is, the death of the 'I' and the liberation of the Other.

It is the 'I' that dies. But it was the 'I' that was made alive. 107
That is how the process of salvation becomes continuous. It is a constant process in which an 'I' is brought to life, and then dies that another 'I' may be brought to life, which in turn dies. The pattern is so consistent in the whole of Scripture that it hardly matters from which example one approaches it first. But Isaiah 52:13-53:12, the Fourth Servant Song, is probably the most familiar expression of this pattern. Higher criticism does not obscure — it rather illuminates — the continuity of the pattern. The image there is of a Servant who, in every possible respect, dies: he dies physically, but he also dies in being despised and rejected and totally deprived of any means of communicating his message. 'Whatever the truth is,' people say, '*that* can't be it.' Only by this process does he come to the point where 'he shall see the fruit of the travail of his soul, and be satisfied' (v 11), where it can be said that 'he shall divide the spoil with the strong.' And if what is written there is written not so much of an individual prophet as of a whole community, then the message is that in order to fulfil its purpose a whole community, the people of Israel, must learn the formula and live by it. It is not a technique for the distinguished ascetic, but a pattern of how the work of God is done.

It hardly needs to be said that this is how Scripture interprets 108
the Crucifixion itself. At the moment when a wholly complete 'I'

appeared in the world — one whom when we had seen we had seen God, as John says — that 'I' had to be destroyed in order that other selves could come to life. And the disciples are not greater than their master: that will be their pattern as it was his. Thus as we have said (§63) Pentecost is the harvest of the Cross. 'It is good for you that I go away.' (John 16:7)

This is how we can think of the Cross without being plunged 109 into despair and into loathing of the human race. As St. Paul said, 'The Son of God, Jesus Christ. . . was not Yes and No; but in him it is always Yes. For all the promises of God find their Yes in him.' (II Cor. 1: 19-20). Among the many other things that this passage — unusually condensed even by Paul's standards — conveys is the affirmation that Christ incarnate is God's 'YES!' exactly in the sense in which the 'YES!' has proved to be the goal of true communication.

Yet the communication — God answered, as it were, in 110 Christ — is in that act of Incarnation only a making visible of what had always been so. A thousand years, remember, are as yesterday: there is no time in God's divine communication at its archetypal point. As soon as there was God, there was the Word (§78). 'Before Abraham was, I AM' (John 8:58). In what sense, then, can we say that God 'died' to produce this 'I' which in turn died to produce the believer's 'I'?

When certain American theologians in about 1966 began to 111 perplex the Christian scene with a theory of the 'Death of God', it can be only this that they were feeling after. If their theology ended in a sort of distorted intellectual evangelicalism, this was because the Formula was, at a critical point, ignored in their thinking. But yes: the only way in which human minds can begin to wrestle with the otherwise totally incomprehensible idea of Creation is to take it the way Scripture takes it. God said, 'Let there be light!': and then, not only was there light, but the light must go on on its own. The light must become energy, it must become the basis of physics. So it is with all manner of life. That which we call 'The Creation' represents God's free gift of independent existence; his sharing of his being; therefore, his renunciation of absolute control of that which he sent out from Himself. As if this were not made clear enough in the first Creation story, the second goes over the ground again and shows the consequences of God's gift of independent judgment as well as independent life. There is no other way of expressing it in human language than to say that in some sense the Creator, in creating, laid down his life. It is certainly true, if we use such language, that we must accept St.

John's limitation: 'No one takes (my life) from me; I lay it down of my own accord.' But that 'I' which, so to put it, could have retained absolute and uncreative omnipotence, extinguished itself, at that precise point, in order to produce a Creation. It would not have been a Creation had it been God's plaything. The Master of the vineyard did not use his vineyard merely to sit about in; he wanted the vineyard to bear grapes: more, he wanted those whom he placed in charge of it to bear the fruits of the Spirit. So he went into a far country (Mark 12:1). In the story the adventure was a failure, and ended in destructive retribution — unless our Lord's ending is understood in the form of a question, 'What will he do? Will he not come and destroy the tenants? Wouldn't you in his place?' The end of the larger cosmic story is not yet told: but its beginning is beyond question.

At least, it is beyond question if we assume, as we here do, that God's purpose was liberation. Scripture, we are arguing, insists that we assume that. In particular, when the Gospels work out the story of the filtering into a mortal time-span of this divine formula of communication and creation, they always insist on it. A particularly eloquent example is the story in St. John 5 in which our Lord heals a cripple and makes him able to walk. The scene is set by the pool of Bethesda, about which John tells us not only that it has five porticoes but that it was the center of a singularly disagreeable and idolatrous superstition. Custom decreed that people should believe that an 'angel' touched the water at certain seasons, and that whoever was mobile enough, or pushing enough, or had the right friends, could be miraculously healed of his complaint if he were the first to be let down into the water. So the unfortunate creature on whom the story focuses is twice a prisoner; he is lamed by his disease, but he is also reduced by the superstition to a condition of whining querulousness. The answer to 'Do you want to be healed?' is not, 'Yes, I do,' but 'It isn't fair: I never get a chance.' Correspondingly what Jesus does for him is done in two stages. He is made mobile (and attracts the unfavorable notice of the authorities by at once getting up and carrying his stretcher on a Sabbath day); and so far as he is concerned all that has happened is that he is now, after nearly forty years of miserable impotence, able to walk. (He does not know who Jesus is). Then, 'afterward', as the story is told, they meet again; and our Lord is represented as congratulating him on his recovery, and then adding, 'Sin no more, that nothing worse befall you.'* In that sentence, what can the words 'sin' and 'worse' mean? 'Worse' surely means to describe the condition of somebody who is sick in both body and mind, and whose body alone has been cured. (The man, now mobile, can spread his infectious self-pity much more efficiently). As for 'sin' — what can this be but the man's settled belief that his disease, and the unpleasantness or superior cunning of his neighbours, were alike sent by God? Of course he believed that. Anyone who believed the nonsense about the angel touching the water and making it healing for whoever jumped the line of waiting pilgrims would believe that God was capable of treating people with tyrannous injustice. Believing it, he would say so. Expanded opportunities of saying so, of spreading a cruel lie about God, are the 'worse thing'. 'Sin' is in deciding to believe exactly what he has been believing.

This is why it would have been fatal had he known at the first 113 stage that his healer (in the physical mode) was Jesus. He would have told everybody — and there would have been ample opportunities after so spectacular a cure — that what God had done to him, Jesus had undone; in other words, that Jesus was God's enemy and conqueror. In the Master's mind this was the most dangerous of all sin's possible products, and once we have seen it here it becomes clear that he was constantly at pains to prevent people making this judgment. In this he could not hope to be wholly successful; short of brainwashing people (a strictly demonic activity which has been named only recently but which tyrants have always known about) this would be impossible. But even though it is John who sees all this most clearly, the Synoptic evangelists not infrequently report Jesus as urging people not to make his great powers too public, or at least not to dramatize the benefits they have personally received. At one surprising and revealing moment he tells somebody who addresses him in the normal fashion, 'Good Master' — perhaps meaning scarcely anything by the adjective — not to call him 'Good' because only God is good. And most dramatically of all, at the Feeding of the Five Thousand, as John tells the story, not only does he take precautions against being chased by the crowd and made there and then

---

*I am not sure that the RSV, which is an unobjectionable translation of the Greek, conveys the required emphasis as well as King James, which reads, 'lest a worse thing befall thee.' The *worse* should not be thought of as being weakened by the 'nothing'; a worse thing is specifically in our Lord's mind.

into a national hero: he follows up his symbolic action by a discourse which says quite precisely, and in terms so explicit as to be almost gruesome, that in order to receive what he is waiting to give, his people must learn to destroy him as food is destroyed before it can nourish.

The whole Gospel story, and perhaps especially the openly 114 miraculous strain in it, is a paradigm of the divine formula. Whatever else one makes of the miracles, they always show us the encounter between a perfect human being and a bent and distorted world. The central Figure is always and uncompromisingly the 'I': the whole and complete being. The encounter is a multiplication, a raising to enormous power, of the pattern on which one could not encounter Jesus in the most casual fashion without being changed — without being brought nearer, even if only in an infinitesimal degree, the design of God which misjudgment and wilfullness had disfigured. And in the performance of these works, or 'signs' as they are so pregnantly described by the evangelists, there was a momentary death in the Saviour. This indeed accumulated into a total death, in as much as it was exactly these manifestations of the 'I', along with all those which were in every word of teaching he gave, that brought down on him the wrath and vengeance of the authorities. One can just hear some member of the Sanhedrin after an early meeting on this emergency, saying as he walked across the temple court, 'The fellow is asking for trouble.' That, like Caiaphas's famous epigram about one man dying for the people, would have been pure prophecy.

There is no doubt that, helpless though they were before 115 Pentecost, the apostles at least got this message. After a very similar incident, in which their post-pentecostal energy communicated itself to a lame beggar at one of the temple gates, Peter is reported as saying to those who crowded round in astonishment, 'Why do you stare at us, as though by our own power or piety we have made him walk?' The first and most natural thing for Peter to say is that this is not their own power, to use as they wish, but God's, to be used at his bidding and for his glory. That means, in less ecstatic language, that it is now the business of the apostles to demonstrate in word and action the one truth which their Master demonstrated — that God loves, and always did love, his world, and to recall as many people as they can reach from the error of the pilgrims at Bethesda, which was to assume that God held it in capricious and tyrannous contempt.

This is, of course, to say that the miracles are patterns of 116 liberation — of deliverance from bondages which go much farther than the physical bondage of disease or bodily malfunction. As Dr. John Marsh has unforgettably said of another very important passage in St. John, the 'miracle of the miracle' in the healing of the blind man (John 9) is in the opening of his spiritual eyes so that he saw and knew who Jesus was, and what his purpose was.* In a parallel story, that of Bartimaeus in St. Mark 10, we hear that the final result of the man's being given his sight was that he 'followed him in the way' (Mk 10:52). Being a follower of Christ was the liberation: it was as much a refreshment and re-creation of the spirit as the giving of sight was to his physical being.

It is necessary, now that we have got so deep into the testimo- 117 nies of Scripture, to digress for a moment from our main argument, and to say, in case any reader is in doubt about the approach to miracle-stories that is here presupposed, that so weighty is the testimony of Scripture in support of the formula of creation, communication, self-renunciation and liberation, that I believe it to be quite safe to doubt a supposed miracle story which does not clearly follow it. It was for this reason that I argued in *The Gift of Conversion* against the authenticity of the story of the cursing of the fig tree in Mark 11: 12-14, 20-23. I follow those who say that it is a parable which has been changed into an anecdote; I further added that it is highly probable that seeing a fig tree with signs already of blight, the Master said, 'We shall see no fruit on that tree' (rather than, 'May no fruit be on it'), that the next day, passing the same tree, a disciple looked at it again in the light of what Jesus had said and saw for himself the signs of blight, and that upon this Jesus based the teaching about faith which ends the story. What I cannot possibly believe is that the Son of God should suddenly act so completely out of character as to curse, out of personal pique, a fig tree that was not bearing fruit in early April. But it is only too believable that on just one or two occasions the affectionate reverence of the disciples caused the parable to be upgraded to the status of a physical miracle, and that their guard was for a moment down. The ascription of irresponsible power to him was exactly what Jesus would have most deeply disapproved, and he wanted nobody to think of him as a worker of capricious miracles for his own convenience. By the same token (as I argued in the same place) I am wholly doubtful about the ascription to Jesus of the destruction of the Gadarene swine. We need not doubt that they did run over the cliff as the story says: so extraordinary an incident is not the kind of thing anybody would

---

*John Marsh, *St. John,* Pelican Commentaries, 1968, pp 387-8

invent. Nor need we doubt a word of the fantastic scene that was being enacted between Jesus and the mad giant in the graveyard. But the idea that Jesus positively willed this to happen seems blasphemously out of character. Destruction is not liberation for anyone. It is the self that is destroyed and rises again: it is the other, the object of communication, who is liberated in order that he may become in turn a liberator through the same cross-centered process.

To my own mind, a similar question should probably be 118 raised about the deaths of Ananias and Sapphira in Acts 5: 1-11. I am far from sure that this story can be used as a model of how the church should behave to people who, for however discreditable reasons, falsify their tithe-returns. The Holy Spirit is not demonstrably present in acts of destruction of this kind. We need not doubt that it happened — Peter was, we know, formidable after Pentecost and if his shadow could heal, his frown could probably endanger a weak heart.

To return, however, to our main argument, we are now in a 119 position to consider the nature of the change brought about by the application of the Formula. In religious terms the change is known as conversion, and I have to say again that in the lost book *The Gift of Conversion* I took a position on this which I still, though if possible more decisively, hold. It is, on my view, precisely what I have been describing as liberation.

The first way of approaching this is to bring out a point which 120 has been implied in the last few pages. The last decade has not yielded very much in theology that is creative, but it has thrown up a considerable enthusiasm for what is called 'the theology of liberation.' All that needs to be said here is that arguments based on this theology can be judged valid or delusive on exactly the standards that applied to the miracle stories. Liberation is not what is claimed but what is given. The apostles at Pentecost did not claim it (they had no idea how they could); but once they received it they knew that there was only one reason why it had been given: that it might be passed on. They knew that just as the archetypal 'I' had died to give it to them, so they must die to give it to others. It might be a physical death in martyrdom; it might be anything from that to what Paul describes as being accursed from Christ that his friends might be saved (Romans 9:3). But it is easy to see how, even when it is given and not claimed, it can be represented simply as the removal of wordly inconveniences and frustrations. This is where it is so important to distinguish the two stages in the liberation of the cripple in St. John 5. (§112-3);

55

liberation which corresponds *only* to the first stage — the removal of the disabilities — makes the liberated more vulnerable to Satan than he was before. It is only too likely that some apostles of 'liberation', prompted by the most generous instincts, will stop at that point in their advocacy. If they do, the consequence will be that the conferrer of liberation will take satisfaction in conferring it and thus evade the responsibility of destroying the 'I'; and that the receivers of it will be content simply to be made able to walk, and not receive it as a gift which will make the same demand of self-destruction. Moreover, it has to be said that one of the great temptations which beset modern theologians is to substitute public breast-beating about the corruption of the institutional church for the death of the 'I'. A 'theology of the servant' is current here and there which should more properly be called the theology of the scullion — or indeed, the theology of the slave: as if the church should be proud of nothing but its shabbiness, and aim at nothing but barbarous mediocrity, and as if this kind of behavior is going to make the church better able to communicate with the underprivileged and the secularized. But all that is a delusion, since the death of the 'I' is the victorious death of a royal and triumphant self.

> Pange, lingua, gloriosi
> praelium certaminis —

That is the keynote, rather than the miserable self-indulgences of piety in the libretto of Stainer's *Crucifixion* and the non-biblical parts of the Bach Passions.

> 'Tis mercy all — the Immortal dies,'

said Charles Wesley in one of his magnificent moments of oxymoron. Those who talk of liberation are handling life and death. Like their Master, they are 'asking for trouble'.

# VI
# Liberation and Life

'The Immortal dies': that has to be the key to any understand- 121
ing of conversion. So let us first consider the immortality which
conversion is designed to generate, remembering all the time that
the subject of this whole essay is the Divine Formula of
communication.

If the reader refers back to §43 he will recall that we have 122
already suggested the identity of conversion and liberation, as
aims which the preacher and the artist alike have in view. Now the
subjective sense of liberation is quite easy to identify. It is, to put it
one way, like the emergence from *status pupillaris* to a status of
full responsibility: like the *ius docendi* which is conferred on
advanced university graduates. The difference between it and its
opposite is the difference between the condition of a person who is
learning to drive a car and that of a person who drives with
confidence; or between that of the pupil who is still searching for
the notes of a piano and the pianist who can play whatever is set
before him.

One very clear mark of that difference is that in the unlib- 123
erated condition one has to think consciously, and make decisions, about every detail of action required to produce the result.
While a car-driver is in that condition, he is a danger on the road
and needs close supervision. Maturity means that he wears the car
as if it were a suit of clothes. It does not deliver him from error: he
may still take wrong decisions and be involved in accidents. But
until he becomes incapable of movement he will not 'forget how to
drive'. He will never have to go through the learning process again
(even if some misdemeanor makes him liable for re-testing, or to
the learning properly of certain principles he never did learn the
first time around). A musician similarly can remember a time
when the playing of the simplest piece was a painful effort — and
when the hearing of it was no less painful to his listener. He may
not remember exactly at what moment he found that he had only

to hear a piece to know what key it was in, or that he could give a decent account of anything in the *Forty Eight Preludes and Fugues*. But there was such a moment of change, and even if he allows his technical facility to lapse, or never develops it very far, he will never again be totally ignorant of the sound represented by a page of music.

From that it seems to follow that the liberated condition 124 implies that there is a great deal less decision-taking than there was in the earlier state. Rather, perhaps, the faculty of decision is left for the work that only it can do, and a great deal that used to be done by painful decision is now done by habit. Again: there is plenty of room for wrong decision (bad driving, perverse interpretation) and plenty of room for laziness to have its way. But the liberated state seems to be one in which doing what needs to be done, in getting the car moving or the piece played, is what comes reasonably naturally. Two theological echoes seem to sound from these notions. One is a reminiscence of the old church controversies about whether there could be sin after baptism; if a Christian really was converted or liberated, could anything put him back to the condition in which Christianity was to him a strange field in which he could walk only with the help of a guide? Or was it that he had been mistaken, and so had his preceptors, in claiming conversion in the first place? That anyhow is the kind of thought that must have exercised the minds of the early Fathers who disputed about this. The other echo is expressible in the old conundrum: of two people who do a good action, one of whom finds it difficult and the other easy, which is the better person? Answer — the second, no matter how unkind that appears to be to the efforts of the first. And this second point happens to be one of immense importance, as we are about to see.

Our chief contention in this essay, be it remembered, is to 125 show that this artist in his communications is allowed to reflect the pattern of God in his; and that the communication work of the church in its preaching and liturgy is artist's work. Therefore we must press on with our description of the liberated condition which we are claiming to be the purpose of all such activity. And one new light on that condition has just begun to make itself visible. Once again we can refer for our authority to the life and teaching of Christ himself.

It is manifest from the Gospels that our Lord was especially 126 at pains to admit his disciples to such knowledge as they could compass of the relation between him and his Father. As disciples they could do no more than listen: as apostles they were to be given the skill to put it into action in their own lives and the lives of others. But from the first our Lord sounded two notes in his example and his teaching which are of the utmost importance.

The first is moral. In St. Matthew 5-7 the heart of his teaching 127 is exposed in a faithful and skillful 'digest' made by the author of that Gospel, known as the Sermon on the Mount. Without lingering over all its delectable details, we can broadly say that those pages of Scripture prescribe a way of life which can be described both as mature (as Dr. Jenkins pointed out in the source referred to in §104) and as *relaxed*. Throughout Chapter 5, which begins with the Beatitudes and ends with the precept of perfection, our Lord is dealing with the difference between the popular interpretation of good behaviour and his own. Firmly insisting that he is not altering a single detail of the moral law that everybody agrees on, he then proceeds to show how that can be interpreted otherwise than as a vexatious bondage. As Matthew reports him, he elsewhere has very stern things to say about those who have by their teaching and example made it a bondage (for example in Chapter 23); but here he seems almost light-heartedly to dismiss the popular and accepted notions of 'law'. The passages about contempt being as pernicious as murder, lust as adultery, levity of speech as perjury, are so cast as to sound as if he were saying, 'Who wants to live a life bounded by a prohibition when he can live one full of the adventure of love?' Go one mile, as you are obliged to: don't waste time and energy protesting about that. But go a second, and something exciting will happen. (The man whose bag you are carrying will ask you why you are doing it: and good conversation could come of that). Turn another cheek and you will surprise your angry assailant — possibly out of his anger. Give more than the beggar asks and you may surprise him out of his grievance. It is the difference between a life spent avoiding positive evil and a life devoted to creating good: and the whole tone of the passage suggests that it is the second which will be happier and, in a very real sense, easier.

The sixth chapter reinforces that from a different angle. Its 128 chief subject is intimacy with God — through prayer, through religious observance, and through a certain attitude to life. Prayer can be made as to a Father who wants to hear his children speak. Religious observance need have none of those trappings which are designed to make other people realize how much effort you are putting into it. And the result will be a life from which the demon of worry has been exorcised.

In Chapter 7, the notion of anxiety is taken a little further. 129

The precept against 'judging' is a precept against anxiety — the anxiety to be a step above one's neighbour, to fuss over specks in his eye. From there we go back to innocent prayer, and at last, and only here, do we enter a dark passage of comparison between this liberated life and the bondage to which the false prophets constantly invite the unwary. It is those who 'do the will of the Father', not those who constantly call on his name, who will be admitted to that Kingdom which all these illustrations have been describing. But more — it is those who do God's will and like doing it who will enter: for the only kind of obedience God is interested in is the obedience of those for whom duty and delight are the same.

It is this condition of simply not *wanting* to do otherwise that 130 marks out the apostle. To do what one believes to be right, and find it constantly vexatious, is to have a mind and spirit angled away from the goal, and to be constantly (as the Lord said to St. Paul on that famous occasion) 'kicking against the goad'. The human consequence of this is to make one's goal, and one's efforts to achieve it, so disagreeable that nobody feels invited to take the same course. One's children, friends or pupils can only be coerced and threatened into conformity: every word such a parent, colleague or teacher says is calculated to put anyone else off for life. But it is not only unpleasant: it is plain illogical. Who will drive a safe car who constantly resents the need to do what is necessary to operate it? Who will play a page of music in a manner fit to listen to who resents what the music demands in terms of discipline and reason? Above all, can one conceive of Mozart writing an opera or a string-quartet with one eye, as it were, constantly over his shoulder to guard against the criticism of some preceptor who will accuse him of breaking this or that rule. He does not want to 'break' any 'rule'. He want his music to live. The artist is he who knows most about the teaching of the Sermon on the Mount.

But Jesus was not of those who have to tell us to do, not what 131 they do, but what they advise. Himself he knew and acted on these principles without a second's remission. What his Father commanded, that above all things he loved. This was as true, surely, in the physical world as in the moral. We read here and there in one or two tender Gospel passages of his manifest distress at the sight of conditions which showed distortions and corruptions of God's physical design for humanity (he was 'moved with pity', Mark 1:41: 'moved with compassion' towards a hungry crowd, Mark 6:34 — they are very strong Greek words); we read similarly of his triumphant recognition of the quality he called 'faith' in the afflicted, which must be interpreted as a desire to see God's design restored ('Do you *want* to be well?'). Parallel to that is his often-expressed disgust at mental corruption, the condition he often called 'hypocrisy', the state of mind of those who called his healing miracles witchcraft. All this seems to indicate that he was himself in total command of all those decisions which preserve and nourish health of body and of mind. Yet, if one thinks of him (as one does) as always radiantly healthy, can anything be more incongruous than thinking of him as 'taking care of his health?' Can one think of him as working out laboriously the answer to some trick question or some trivial and dangerous comment, and saying that he must have notice of the question, or reserving his judgment? These are reactions and habits which, to speak humanly, 'came naturally.' And this, if it is rightly argued, confirms the point we are here making, that the whole of his life and teaching are really summed up in the most astonishing call to action ever issued by any leader: 'Come to me, all who labour and are heavy laden, and I will give you rest.'

That, if one wants it in a sentence, is humanity's charter of 132 liberation. Here are sheep without a shepherd, here are people whose minds and often whose very bodies are distorted out of all recognition by a heritage of wrong decisions: here they are, weighed down by the burden of believing that God does not love the world; walking like men with club feet, clumsily; like the blind, hesitantly; like the paralyzed, painfully. Our Lord does not say, 'Try harder'; he does not talk about blood and tears and sweat (those will be his to bear): when he is talking about the Kingdom, the design of God, it is in terms of getting rid of burdens, not of taking up a cross. Taking up a cross is, when he does come to it late in his ministry, accepting the death of the 'I', the creative death that will liberate the Holy Spirit and set others free to take up theirs. It is, in the light of that, hard to have patience (not only hard, but plain wrong) with hymns, prayers, liturgies and Christian habits, which represent Jesus as a gloomy and overbearing prophet whose good news is contingent on the acceptance of a mournful life and a heart-choking self-immolation. What burdens life offers will become easy to carry if one can stand up straight and carry them on the yoke made by the best of carpenters.

The purpose of the communication of the Good News, then, 133 is to produce this condition in people, and the mark of the 'converted' is the light-hearted acceptance of the yoke — itself not the yoke of the defeated but the yoke that makes the burdens light. Now when, many pages back, we said that the purpose of preaching in the church's liturgies is liberation, it was exactly this that we were saying. We can now go over that ground again and make the point more forcibly.

In two ways the Church in its communications makes use of 134 the arts: of rhetoric in preaching, and, more comprehensively, of drama in liturgy. It will now be a little clearer, perhaps, that these arts can be neglected or misued, and that there are standards by which we may judge when that is happening. The purpose in view must always be the generating in worshipers of some kind of conversion: but false ideas of what conversion is distort the whole activity of worship, and it is against these that we must use what weapons of intellect and insight we have.

For it is at this point that we must bring back into our picture 135 the proposition we made back in §79-80 that the liberation will not take place if we the liberators attempt to control it. This is the point at which the church needs to learn from the artists. The Donne poem (§34) is a perfect example of the impact of an artist's work: but the impact has nothing to do with the poet's decision. We said that. It seemed harmless when we said it of Donne. Does it look so harmless when we say it of the church's efforts at evangelism? The artist knows all about the extinction of the 'I'; does the Church?

This is where the divine paradox appears in all its fierceness. 136 The whole purpose of a 'conversion' is to generate a fully-grown 'I': as near a perfect 'I' as can be achieved. This is what Paul calls the 'fulness of the stature of Christ', or 'Christ in me'. But in so far as there is a human agency assisting in this, there is a point, as we have shown, where that human agency extinguishes its 'I'; and we have also said that the converted person is not merely a receiver but a transmitter of this new kind of life, ('zoe' in St. John), and therefore must be ready to extinguish, for the liberation of others, the 'I' which has been so triumphantly aroused. Death comes before resurrection, and the resurrection of my 'I' is in you, not in me. The point about to be argued is that the Church, in its evangelism, must be as objective about this as the poet and the musician naturally are; and we shall have to say that at this point church people are often quite remarkably unfaithful.

It can be added that this is a condition in the church which 137 can be discerned at any period of its history, even if different periods have produced it in different modes. The story of Simon Magus in Acts 8 is relevant and illuminating here. In the first half of that chapter we read that one of the less talked-about apostles,

62

Philip, entered on a ministry in Samaria — an awkward assignment, no doubt. It seems that he encountered a powerful personality, Simon, who was in the habit of drawing attention to himself as a healer of some kind. Simon offered to become his assistant, or maybe his publicity officer, having seen that Philip's preaching was receiving more favour than his own. A cunning ellipsis on the part of the narrator (I cannot see it otherwise) allows us to imagine that news of the remarkable success of this partnership reached the council of apostles in Jerusalem and that they found it disturbing. Peter went and visited Samaria, and was at once approached by Simon (whom we can imagine speaking in a kindly but patronizing manner about Philip) and asked by him what fee Peter would take for sharing the secret of the Holy Spirit with him; to which Peter replied (as J.B. Phillips translated him in one of his inspired moments), 'To hell with you and your money.' The sin of Simon was complex but is painfully familiar. For him religion was, undoubtedly, a matter of programming people into health and obedience. It could, he saw, become a remarkably successful business enterprise if somebody as down-to-earth as Peter, rather than the head-in-the-clouds idealist Philip, were promoting it. It all sounds mournfully reminiscent of certain religious enterprises nearer our own time and place.

But it is a first-class example of the difference between the Gospel and the pseudo-Gospel. It is interesting that when we next (and last) hear of Philip he becomes the founder of the Coptic Church through a mere accident, an encounter with a high Ethiopian official whom he will never see again, in a country that is not Ethiopia.

It might be fair to say that the heretics and trouble-makers we hear of in the New Testament were all tarred with this brush. It is even conceivable that not Simon Magus, but Judas Iscariot, was the real archangel of the 'programming' heresy. It is conjecture, but perhaps not wholly groundless conjecture, that he whose qualities seemed to fit him to be treasurer of the disciples' group (John 12:6) and whose major temptations were economic, might have a fatal touch of philistinism in his soul. He might well have applied his disastrous words, 'To what purpose is this waste?' not only to Mary's gesture but to the strategy of his Master, and turned away from him a disappointed, and then in the end a treacherous, disciple. It may be so: one certainly cannot believe that our Lord did not see that kind of thing coming from Judas or from elsewhere.

What I have slipped into calling by the disagreeable word 140
'programming' is the activity which refuses to extinguish the 'I'
and which therefore refuses to countenance the liberation of the
person to whom the Gospel is to be communicated. This suggests
that we shall encounter the disorder both at an organizational and
at a psychological level. Therefore we must turn at once to the
public activities of the church, from which we shall then find our
way back into the field of aesthetics.

# VII

## Temptations of Organizers

'Programming' can be expressed, in terms of the analogy in    141
§29 above, as taking precautions against the dropping of the ball.
Therefore one aspect of it will certainly be, in the church's life,
organizational. The figure was worked out in §§44-5 in terms of
'tradition', and it was there suggested that tradition must contain
an element of risk. When people talk, as they constantly and
exasperatingly do, about tradition as if it were always dead tradition or oppressive tradition (or, come to that, a tradition they
don't personally like), they are overlooking this vital distinction.
The active principle of a living tradition is risk — the death of the
'I' in the most literal sense of being the death of the person who
handed the deposit of tradition to the other person: the death of
the preceptor who must be replaced by the candidate. We said or
suggested that, and now it becomes clear that the church will
always be vulnerable to the temptation improperly to guard its
tradition.

Any criticism of church order is really a suggestion that this    142
has happened: that at some point tradition has become a bondage
instead of a liberation. Such criticism will be responsible when it is
undertaken with a full recognition that corrupt tradition is not the
only kind of tradition. I will therefore give a very simple and
almost trivial example which may serve to pry open a rather
awkward lock. Recently at a very famous center of church music
in the United States, where public worship is valued and well
attended, a new hymn was introduced at the commencement
service — which, as in all such institutions, is a highly ceremonious and emotive occasion. It was, and deserved to be, a massive
success.* When subsequently sung on College occasions through

---

*It was 'Rejoice, ye pure in heart' (a poorish text) as set by Richard
Dirksen in 1974, *Westminster Praise* #1; it is arguably one of the six
greatest tunes composed in the 20th century so far for a hymn.

the next year it continued to endear itself to the worshiping body and abruptly achieved the status of a 'favorite hymn' or a 'chart hitter'. A very wise and perceptive student, who was a member of the committee proposing the program for the following year's Commencement, reported that their committee had again chosen this hymn, but went on to say, 'We'd like to see this hymn as a permanent part of Commencement services.' Now this was not the sort of trivial hymn that so often does become an overnight 'winner'; it is a stroke of genius. But even so, that rider was misconceived and the fact had to be pointed out. Full of the authentic thrill of having heard and enjoyed this particular piece, what the students were saying was, 'We want to be sure that this delight is passed on to every future generation.' Could anything be more admirable, when a genuinely fine piece of music was in question? Yet this is what we must not do, because a little thought indicates what the consequences will be: ten years after, the hymn will lose all those qualities which aroused its first hearers. It will become, in the popular use of the word, a 'formality'. It will no longer do what it did for those who first heard it if it becomes, to use another popular phrase, a 'rubber stamp' insertion into a ceremony.

Now is this to say that all ceremonies that have become tradi- 143 tional, or all things which, in some forms of worship, always happen, are to be uprooted, and that everything which has been done three times would then be left undone? Manifestly not, because there are other traditional units in worship which do not lose their power through the passing of the years. Let us take, by contrast, any formal Collect from the Book of Common Prayer, such as that associated in the old liturgies with the Fourth Sunday after Trinity:

> O God, the Protector of all that trust in thee, without whom nothing is strong, nothing is holy: increase and multiply upon us thy mercy that, thou being our ruler and guide, we may so pass through things temporal that we finally lose not the things eternal. Grant this, O heavenly father, for Jesus Christ's sake, our Lord.

Let us disdain such distractions as concern the use of archaic language in the modern church, and admit that this has, historically, done four hundred years' good work in nourishing the devotion of at least one significant section of the Church. If there is any case for removing it or replacing it, it does not rest on the arguments which would dislodge the Dirksen hymn tune from liturgical invariableness. No: the reason why that was and remained beautiful is precisely that it was never primarily intended to be beautiful. It is a translation of a much older Latin prayer, and Cranmer, translating it, was concerned only to produce a translation into good English. The original Latin author meant no more than to produce a composition in a form (the Collect form) as restricted and disciplined as that of a sonnet. There was no question here of passing on a great thrill; it was a question only of passing on an expression of truth. Nobody, in the transmission of that prayer, said, 'This is so lovely: we must insist that everybody else share it.' We have only a medieval monk doing his duty and a Reformed Archbishop doing his. The decisions taken have nothing to do with what later generations will *feel*: they have nothing to do with precautions against their missing the message. For the deadly temptation in all such moments of exaltation is to behave as Peter did at the Transfiguration. 'Let us camp here for ever'. The moment he said that, the vision faded.

The area in which we are moving at this moment is organizational. It is very much a matter of making choices *about* communication, not of creative communication itself. The students were not writing that hymn, they were choosing it, using it: and it is just here, where something has moved *us* to exaltation, that we have to guard most vigilantly against the error of Peter on the mountain. 144

In the broader and more palpable matter of institutional organization itself, the same principle tends to apply. It is illiterate to claim that no church needs an institution, or that once the church become visible it becomes corrupt. Fashionable calumnies about the institutional church are always trivial. But it is hardly more responsible to claim that once an institution is sacred it is immune from temptations that assail others. On the contrary, it is vulnerable to all the temptations that banks or finance trusts or even universities are little worried by, and others besides. Crude temptations associated with power have brought up their batteries against the church in the past, and still do. If one wants to distinguish between the corrupt and the innocent use of power and influence, one can do worse than ask to what extent the power is being used to protect or to enshrine what it is not our duty to protect. In this area, since I am not writing and should never aspire to write a book about ecclesiastical politics, I am content to bring in only such evidence as serves the present argument. 145

But it does look as if that episode of Ananias and Sapphira to which we have already referred (§118) is a bad guide for church administration. We need not claim that Peter murdered those two; we profoundly hope that he did not desire, and was horrified 146 by, their deaths. But clearly the use of any sort of violence to enforce Christian belief is a major violation of our doctrine of 'no precautions'. Even if we deplore the dogmatic permissiveness of the present age, nobody wants the Inquisition back, even for disciplinary purposes, let alone as a support for the orthodox Creed. We may not say, 'Break these divine laws and we will punish you, even kill you.' Indeed, the most amiable illustration of the right approach to this that I know is the epigram coined by an obviously very wise headmaster addressing the newest arrivals at his school*, when he said, 'If you break my rules, God help you; if you break God's rules, I'll help you.' Yes: there must be human justice — that is a greater social need than some at present admit —but in the area in which the Church does its work, you operate on a very different scale.

One must suppose that the Reformation debates were very 147 largely centered on the question of what the Church through its institutions is entitled to control and what it is not entitled to control. Luther's whole argument about Justification by Faith turns on a protest against the church's attempts to control *that*. If he said (as he assuredly did) that that is a matter between the believer and his God, he was saying that it was something about which the church's organization could do nothing, and that where they tried to do anything they were in grave error. The subsequent controversies which engaged the English during the seventeenth century were basically pivoted on the question of what any Church could regard itself as entitled to do with people's lives: was the Church in England to be prelatical or not? Were prelates ever entitled to invoke secular strength to enforce conformities? Did people approach God through bishops, through presbyters, or through a common consensus of the kind advocated by the Quakers and the Independents of the mid-seventeenth century? These disputes in the end generated visible bodies of opinion, each with its own tradition and regulations and (except the Society of Friends) ministry and written Confession. In turn these bodies had to search themselves constantly to discover how and when they were infringing the principle they had stood for: and when they stopped searching, the enemies of liberation at once noticed it and won back some of the ground the original Reformers had gained from them.

So much is obvious, and a little later we shall amplify its 148

---

*Passed on to me, like so much else that is treasurable, by my old preceptor, Dr. John Marsh implications. But are we saying then that there were no points at which the Church stands fast against false doctrine? Is it all, in the headmaster's words, a matter of God's rules and never a matter of justice controllable by human decision? Not at all, and for exactly the reasons we have already suggested. The church, as an organization, must constantly be under the stress of debate. It must decide painful questions of discipline, and wrestle with deep questions of doctrine. It must, in fact, constantly exercise reason.

This is something about which King Solomon was clearer    149
than some Christians. In the Jewish religious system, justice and the divine revelation were inseparable, and the Temple was a house of justice as well as of devotion; in confirmation of which see the opening paragraph of Solomon's intercession as reported in II Kings 8 and II Chronicles 6. The habitual thinking of Christians is angled so far away from justice and reason that one would be surprised to hear such a sentiment uttered at the dedication of a modern church building. None the less, justice and fairmindedness are part of the essential equipment of any body of Christian people precisely because it is in this area of communication that people must and may make decisions. Just as good law preserves and nourishes true freedom, so good conversation and the courtesies of rational debate nourish doctrine and devotion. Those who accept the prohibition on taking decisions in the wrong area, and who allow themselves to 'program people' not only become tyrants; they miss those 'secondary explosions' (§79) which are the delight of good conversation. Without justice there is neither freedom nor inspiration. This is where the church works out her problems. It is not in taking precautions against the possibilities of problems arising, but in debating problems according to reason, that the Church carries on this part of its work: and it is carried on not only in academic discussions at a high intellectual level, but whenever a Christian opens his or her mouth in the presence of another.

Traditionally the church has been so much occupied in her    150
public speech with ideas and images which are the best vehicles we have for mortal expression of infinite ideas that very often this duty of being precise and obedient in the realm of intellect has been overlooked. In history the most perceptive advocates of this need and practitioners of this technique were the Scholastics and the Puritans, and both were strictly minority groups. It was St. Thomas Aquinas who said, 'Love proceeds from the Word' and Thomas Goodwin who said, 'Our greatest sins are sins of the mind.' But most of their contemporaries would have been happy

to talk about the primariness of Love and the heinousness of sins of the flesh.

This process of reason, this daily obedience to the ongoing 151 demands of The Word (which of course is the preoccupation of the inspired and devoted author of Psalm 119) corresponds, in the artist's work, with the labour and sweat of process II, as described above in §78. In the process of communication there was the initial explosion, and there was the transmission of this to the second party, but between them there was the hard work of what we called incarnation. The Incarnation is described by St. John precisely as the incarnation of the Word; and this is exactly the point in the process we are looking at at this moment. The principle of the Word is not inspiration or beauty but *reason,* and whereas it is forbidden for us to try to control the process by which it becomes apprehended as beauty or delight, it is equally our duty to control the process by which the initial idea becomes expressible. The ongoing conversation of the Church, through which all its decisions are taken, is this process, and subject always to reason.

This means that unless the principle of reason is accepted 152 throughout the field in which the discourse is running, the process will break down. And that happens to be a risk which in most ages was, and in ours pre-eminently is, very high indeed. We are, we recall, comparing the wrong kind of decision-making by a church organization (which could end in the burning of a heretic) with the right kind, which we say must be suject to reason and remain so subject. And we have only to think how difficult it is to get any group of people discussing a matter of religious interest to discuss it objectively to see how high the risk is. Where an issue is being discussed at a domestic level, by, as it were, amateurs in debate rather than trained lawyers, the danger of the whole framework breaking down under the stress of personal feelings is often inescapable. When the times are such that in the secular world the fabric of reason and justice (which normally is what the secular world builds far better than the religious people do) begins to show sings of cracking, the danger is even greater, though the duty is identical.

In the early centuries of Church History decisions on intellec- 153 tual matters were taken by leaders whom we now call the Fathers, who spoke and wrote in Greek and Latin. Those first five centuries are a pageant of painful debates on such issues as the relation between the Son and the Father, the treatment of people who have lapsed from the Church, and the place of free will in human nature. It should not be overlooked that although the parties to this dispute were people whom modern Protestants would probably describe patronizingly as passionate Latins (some of them were swarthy North Africans), most of them had been trained as lawyers and knew and valued the precise meanings of words. It is not easy to give lyric expression to one's thoughts about these titanic debates, but the remarkable English poet Frederick Pratt Green succeeded in doing so:

> How long and earnestly the Fathers strove
> to frame in words a Faith we cannot prove:
> but oh, how dead our creeds
> unless they live in Christlike words and deeds*

Decidedly so: and the Creeds will remain dead if they do not become living expressions of the 'YES!' by one living 'I' after another; but they will never make that effect if they have not been wrought out by the use of reason and the courtesy of debate.   154

One or two illustrations show how strange this sounds to Christians who are brought up without an appreciation of the need for 'justice in the second process.' One would be the number of dubious decisions in areas having a common boundary with international politics of which the Church has been guilty during the present ecumenical age. The very long period between the end of the medieval era and the foundation of the World Council of Churches, in which the Church once again emerged, if not as a world power at least as an international voice, allowed rust to accumulate on the Church's tools of diplomacy, and one did hear justifiable complaints of the unintended embarrassments caused by well-meaning pronouncements from that body in its earliest years to people who were trying to live the Christian life in countries where it was placed under special stress. But nearer home, churchmen who find their way into political debate through journalism or the other media have not been notable for being wiser in their generation than the 'children of darkness.' Sentimentality has fairly often been chargeable against ecclesiastical ventures into the political field.   155

The other most familiar illustration of this defect is the tendency of church organizations to form large Assemblies for the purpose of government and administration, and then, through a false fear of 'legalism', to permit these to become arenas for demagoguery. The large Assembly needs to be very tightly controlled by rules of debate comparable to those in any civilized   156

---

*From *26 Hymns,* 1971, by F. Pratt Green. *Westminster Praise* #11.

Parliament; where people are resentful of such control, the lure of the multitude proves fatal to those of free tongue: and since the forum is so largely composed of preachers, the temptation is intensified.*

Given the Formula, it is easy to understand how reason, worked out in the courtesies and restraints of civilized debate, liberates the truth. Such debate must walk a tight rope from which it can always fall off into oppressive oligarchy on the one hand or demagogy on the other. What used to be called by the eloquent name of sacerdotalism operates equally freely where the powerful govern without consultation or when they govern by appeal to mass-emotion.

157

---

* In this connection is is perhaps worth noting what happened when the United Reformed Church was formed in England (and a small part of Wales) in 1972. One of its constituent bodies, the Congregational Church, had had an annual deliberative Assembly whose full membership was nearer 3,000 than 2,000, and broadly speaking it was this Assembly's duty to interpret the mind of local churches, all of whom sent delegates to it, to the church as a whole. The other body, the Presbyterian Church of England, had a much smaller Assembly, which again broadly speaking, interpreted the mind of its constituent presbyteries, but which then took decisions binding on the local churches. In the details of its behaviour the smaller Assembly was more ceremonious than the larger, and less vulnerable (though not wholly invulnerable) to the impact of demagogic personalities. At the joining of the two bodies both Assemblies were replaced by a body of about 750 members which took over very largely the ceremonious behaviour and language of the Presbyterians. One of the 'creaks' that this adjustment produced was a querulous note among ex-Congregationalists about the legal language and such ceremonies as bowing to the Moderator and the robing of chief executives. There has however been much less shouting in the new Assembly than Congregationalists were used to in their old one.

# VIII

## Temptations of Preachers

But we are now ready to move back into the specific ecclesias-  158
tical area of preaching, an activity for which during the past
generation few people have had a good word to say. The reasons
for the bad press it has received have much to do with the argument we have been following. People about sixty years old now
can remember the time when in the Reformed sections of the
English-speaking churches the preacher was still very widely
respected, and when much was expected of him. When all possible
allowance has been made for his exposure, and consent, to professional temptations, it is fair to say that he often delivered an
excellent product.* Various external forces operated to dethrone
the traditional nonconformist preacher of the period 1850-1930.
Among them was the ecumenical movement, which naturally
exposed denominations of intensely professional traditions to the
values of others whose emphases were in very different places.
Another was the vigorous, if often confused, liturgical interest
which arose in all the English (and not much later, American)
churches from the thirties onwards. A third was the effect of
World War II in dislodging so many assumptions about the
authority of public statements and large-scale oratory from the
minds of many who were led by the iniquities of corrupt politicians to distrust almost anything upon which more than two or
three people agreed.

It has been interesting, and a little unnerving, to notice how in  159
recent times the only preachers who have had anything like the
fame enjoyed by people like Robertson and Spurgeon in other
days have been preachers who operate not from local churches but
on television networks or as free-lance evangelists. I have not

---

*One cannot think otherwise after reading that interesting and somewhat
nostalgic study of the art, written by an author within that tradition but
after its decline, *Varieties of English Preaching,* by Horton Davies.

73

personally tested this, but I think it probable that if one asked ten people in a London street to name any preacher they regarded as eminent, they would, unless one of them happened to be a regular churchgoer (but even then he might not name his own pastor) mention a well known evangelist from North Carolina. In Scotland and Wales it may not be quite so certain yet, and in America one might get three answers rather than one. But it is other kinds of folk-artist who enjoy the attention of the large majority of lay people.

It is, I hasten to say, quite false to say that faithful preaching 160 has disappeared from England. Preaching of the kind I am going to commend is probably flourishing even there as well as it ever did — conceivably better. Only those who hear it know about it —but this again I am not about to regard as a sign that it is failing. And whereas it was at one time possible for a nonconformist sermon-taster to get away with the patronizing comment that if an anglican preached decently that happened by accident, that is a much less safe remark to make now.

But what really concerns us is the relation between preaching 161 and evangelism. For we are asking what the nature of the preacher's communication is. We went into this to some extent back in §38-43, claiming that it was at least comparable to the work of the artist, and we said in §86 that the preacher is a folk-artist. We further showed what weaknesses could appear in the preacher's handling of his craft of communication (§§83-91). But we can now say with more conviction and less appearance of speculation that this folk-artist is required to be the most shining of all examples of the death of the 'I'.

Yes, we have already said even this (§88); but what we then 162 said applied to the main task of the preacher, which is 'preaching to the converted.' He hopes to arouse in each hearer some form of 'YES!' which is personal to that hearer. He is not presenting the Gospel for the first time when he is preaching within the liturgy. He is reminding people of it. He is nourishing in them a hunger which constantly comes week by week. It is not that they have fallen badly short of Christian standards during the week, but rather than they are engaged in a process of gradual growth, which is nourished by the periodic proclamation of the Gospel. This kind of preaching can be done only in the House of Faith; it must· presuppose a certain deposit both of faith and of knowledge in the hearer. For this reason it can be presented quite briefly. A sermon as part of a liturgy should not run the length of the main address in an evangelistic crusade, and indeed the American custom of holding campus services which, slotted as they are into a busy academic timetable, provide for addresses of from four to seven minutes, can be an admirable example of the value of brief liturgical addresses — besides being a most salutary discipline upon preachers who normally claim the right to be more expansive.

This kind of preaching is, in the best traditions, biblical and 163 liturgical: that is, it presupposes at least that the hearer reads and to some extent enjoys the Bible and that the hearer knows more or less where he is in the Church's Year. No more need be presupposed or said explicitly; the hearer should be able, by merely following the preacher's example, to get on his wavelength.

But if it be said that these very obvious remarks apply only to 164 liturgical preaching, to preaching as an instrument of sanctification, and not to preaching as evangelism, that is where I take issue. I do not for a moment believe that the first evangelistic statements of the Aposles were in any sense different from the only preaching I recognize. What were these apostolic sermons? They were passionately-believed statements of an historical fact and of its rational consequences, designed to call forth the work of the Holy Spirit in their hearers.

Let us look at it more closely. The first Apostolic preaching, 165 as recorded in The Acts, was directed to Jews. Arguing in the only terms which would make connection with the religion and intelligence of such people, the apostles said (as the late C.H. Dodd classically showed in his book *The Apostolic Preaching,* but as anybody who reads The Acts can see for himself) that Jesus Christ, a Jew, crucified as a result of a Jewish conspiracy, was alive; that everything written in their Scriptures (the Old Testament) pointed to this if they were properly read; and that therefore they must radically alter their outlook and values if they were to enjoy the fruit of this good news. This was plain statement, it was reasoned argument, and it did indeed communicate to many people (though by no means to all) a new sense of liberation.

Now notice what happened when Peter was faced with what 166 was to him one of his most embarrassing moments. His belief certainly was that just as the people of Israel had generated, in the physical sense, the Saviour of the world, so it would be through that same people that the purpose of God, now understood in its fulness, would be worked out to the end. But one day he was required to meet a thoroughly sincere and respectable Roman colonel who had given every possible evidence that he really wanted to join those who had received the News. Acts 10 describes graphically the dream that Peter had which resolved his dilemma. It was (and we can know it only because he shortly recounted it to all his colleagues) a vision designed to persuade him that 'uncleanness', the principle of separation between Jew and Gentile, was a matter entirely of God's judgment, and that anything human beings had done to set up this principle, for however good and sensible reasons in their time, could be and was now being overridden by God. God decided what could not enter the Church, so Peter need not worry. In consequence Peter received and baptized Cornelius and all his household. But we have no record at all of Peter's saying to Cornelius just what he had always said to the Jews. He cannot possible have said to Cornelius, 'You were wrong' in the sense that he said to the nation that crucified Jesus, 'You were wrong.' No: Peter is on record only as saying (Acts 10:47), 'Can anyone forbid water for baptizing these people who have received the Holy Spirit just as we have?'

That is a doubly astonishing comment; not only because of the change of mind it indicates in Peter, but because it seems to present him, the church's first director of evangelism, as recognizing the work of the Holy Spirit in somebody whom he had only just met, and who was not yet an accredited Christian. There is no assumption here that Cornelius must, under Peter's tuition, abolish everthing he was committed to. No: however it had happened, the Holy Spirit, the liberated condition, was already there, and all Peter and the Church need do was to recognize it. There indeed is a magnificent abandonment of precaution against the dilution of the Gospel!

That is one episode: one has intimations of dozens of others in the letters of Paul, the church's most distinguished free-lance evangelist. Paul, of course, saw as soon as Peter did, and much earlier in his own Christian life, that a good deal of the legal scaffolding that had made the world safe for the Jewish faith could now come down. He knew that Peter had been shaky about this, and did much, by plain speaking, to hearten Peter on occasions when the assurance of his new position on this matter deserted him (Galatians 2 goes into this very carefully). But in his letters we have the classic example of how a man of a single and unshakeable conviction would argue that conviction into the minds and hearts of correspondents all over the civilized world — Celts in 'Galatia' (Turkey), Greeks in Corinth, Latins in Rome — writing always with eloquence but even more with ruthless reasoning, celebrating the Resurrection, presenting the patriarch Abraham in a fashion totally understandable to people who had not been brought up on

167

168

76

Genesis. He was a supreme artist, even if some of his passages are as demanding as a late Beethoven first movement or some passages in the *Art of Fugue,* and what he said to those people remains immortally relevant to all people. But this was exactly because he was an artist: he did not indulge in 'in group' language; he did not enfold people in his own personal sphere of influence. Who can deny to him a sense of humor (one true sign of personal objectivity) after reading II Corinthians 10, especially the passage where he says, "I know what you are saying: he writes eloquent letters but he bores us when he is with us and anyhow he is a comic looking fellow." (Paul, one may say, writing to those pious reprobates, doesn't know whether to laugh or cry; but by the time he gets to II Corinthians 12 he is laughing in heaven).

As if that were not enough, at one point he lays it firmly on the line: this is at the very beginning of what we know as his First Letter, where he reproves the Corinthian church for allowing itself to be split into factions by the eloquence of preachers: they form the Peter party and the Apollos party and the Paul party, and even (heaven help them) the Christ party: and Paul says in exasperation, "Thank God I only baptized two of you." The last thing he personally wanted was for them to be in that sense dependent on him. The thing for whose achievement he could wish himself "accursed from Christ" if need be was that his fellow-Jews should see for themselves the truth of the Gospel; and he would have said that equally about people of any race.

Mention of Apollos reminds us of that very odd and entertaining episode that spans the end of Acts 18 and the beginning of the following chapter. It is there that the Ephesian ministry of Apollos is judged, for all its brilliance, a failure. Luke, writing his account, has gathered that Apollos was indeed "instructed in the way of the Lord: fervent in the spirit, teaching diligently the things concerning Jesus, though he knew only the baptism of John." He is abruptly judged, and judged twice. Aquila and Priscilla, the archetypes of those informed lay Christians whom any minister ignores at his peril, tell him over lunch that it was an excellent and moving sermon but not the Gospel; and when Paul later arrives and asks the Ephesian church wehether it has "received the Holy Spirit", he get a blank stare and a reply, "We have never heard of it. What is it?" It was indeed John the Baptist who said that not he but the Christ, who was on his way, would baptize them with the Holy Spirit; John could evoke only interested questions — the Messiah alone would evoke the 'YES!' John would die for his convictions; only Jesus would die for the world. And here it is

169

170

77

again: a preacher evoking admiration, but no 'YES!' A preacher leaving his people entertained, but as helpless as he found them. This is not as bad as Simon Magus, but it still is not evangelism.

There was, we have to say, plenty of inept evangelism about 171 at that early date, as there has always been since. The temptation to preserve the communicator's 'I', so that people must run back to him time after time for instruction instead of scattering full of the Holy Spirit's enterprise and alertness, was too great for such as Apollos. And indeed had it not been for Paul's laborious working-out of all this in the central chapters of Romans, we might never even yet have seen what the Holy Spirit is waiting to do for us. For could he have put it more persuasively than he does in Romans 8 — after drawing that unforgettable picture of the enslaved condition of a religious man who has no Holy Spirit, no 'YES!' in him ('O wretched man that I am, who shall deliver me from this body of death?', Romans 7:24)? Between that and the triumphant ending of Chapter 8 is an account of the way in which the Holy Spirit establishes intimacy between man and God — teaching him to pray, giving him confidence and self-respect and courage, arousing in him the timeless 'YES!'

Look what has happened. We are skipping from place to 172 place in the profoundest writings of the greatest of all Christian thinkers, and saying just enough, perhaps, to recall to the reader how profound they are. But they are written not for theological students or for experienced Christians, but for people who are infants in the Faith. They are not, perhaps, precisely evangelism since we know that at least some of them were written to churches already established. Yet in what sense was the Ephesian church established when it 'had no Holy Spirit'? In what sense was the Corinthian church, that bunch of ecclesiastical strong-arm men and women, established? What sense were the Romans making of Christianity, to evoke the second half of Romans 1 from Paul? If it was not virgin soil, it was weed-grown soil, and Paul was, as he said, planting in it (1 Corinthians 3:6) what had not been there before.*

---

* Was Paul's university sermon at Athens (Acts 17) a failure? It certainly looks as if this was a place in which Paul evoked no particularly explosive response: and if Luke rightly reports what he said, it was very unusual in him to give such an address without mentioning the name of Christ (referring to him only once, obliquely, as 'a man whom (God) has appointed.') He took a very different line at Corinth, which was his next place, where on his first visit he sought to present to them nothing but 'Christ and him crucified.' (1 Cor. 2:2) The Athenian address is the only

Now if Peter and Paul were so concerned, in their propaga- 173 tion of the Gospel, to send people away with the Spirit in their hearts rather than to draw people towards themselves, who are we to behave differently? We have probably said enough to make it clear that the preacher's most clamorous temptation is to ensure that he himself sees the results of what he has done. A teacher is entitled to see such results, but not a preacher. Our Lord, congratulating his disciples on what must have been a very small-scale experiment in evangelism during his lifetime, must have warmed their hearts when he said (as Luke reports in his chapter 10) 'I saw Satan fall like lightning from heaven.' But he at once added, 'Nevertheless, do not rejoice in this, that the spirits are subject unto you; but rejoice that your names are written in heaven.' The spirits there are no doubt the demons; but it is not beyond the wit of Satan to devise means of tempting us to make the Holy Spirit Himself subject to us.

I am myself tempted to distinguish between the kind of 174 modern evangelism which issues in a long procession of penitents or converts towards the preacher and the other sort of preaching which results in their scattering to do the Lord's work each in his own place. That is, I should concede, not quite fair. We cannot issue a blanket-condemnation of all evangelists in terms like that — though my contention would be that if, or in as much as, any evangelist really thinks his work is done when people walk towards him at the end of a crusade-session, he is in grave error. Indeed, this is not the place to condemn the custom known in America as the 'altar call,' artificial though it too often is. If 'evangelical preaching' has the effect of arousing in a believer a sense that he personally wants at once to make a physical response, it has to that extent aroused the 'I'. So has the preaching of a black preacher, who hopes for, and always gets, articulated responses of 'Amen' and 'Alleluia' and even, precisely, 'YES!' from his congregation, and allows his eloquence to be fed by such responses. But even in such a delicate area as this, we still have to say that the real purpose of preaching, whether it is evangelical or whatever the opposite of that is (I am getting tired already of the distinction), is to evoke the 'I' in the receiver, and at that moment

place where he is on record as saying (and indeed inventing the phrase), 'a funny thing happened to me on the way here.' My personal belief is that for once his sense of humor, sparked off by the shrine to the Unknown God, caused his judgment to falter: so important do I believe the celebration of Paul as a man who could be put off his stroke by something he found comical that I dare to record this belief here.

to evoke the readiness for that 'I' to be crucified for the benefit of some other person whom the believer knows and the preacher does not know; the excitement of the evangelical service must not become subject to the heresy of Peter on the mountain — a thrill to be treasured, a talent to be buried. And the kind of preaching technique which brings the preacher too far forward and obscures the reality he is presenting is pernicious because it is infectious; being over-concerned with the producing of a visible reaction in the hearer, it can induce in the hearer a passivity which is wholly unapostolic.

It is not surprising that in communities where this habit is 175 cultivated exclusively, churches are formed which, while they rejoice in a very high internal voltage of devotion, turn out to be strangely inflexible in their attitudes to their apostolate in the world. It is unfortunate that the word 'evangelical' is normally used to distinguish customs of this sort. But there are two ways in which this principle illustrates itself in the life of the church, both of which are especially to be found in America, but which repeat themselves wherever Christians are found.

The churches of the Southern Appalachian Valleys in the 176 United States certainly provide one example. In those regions communities are ingrown and self-sufficient and small and education is neither vigorous nor highly valued. As a study of these communities puts it:

> A positive religious value is also related in community members' minds to low educational status. Preachers are 'hurt more than helped', according to them, by going to seminary.*

In those communities, according to the authority I quote, education and worldly success are alike feared and suspected. So the last thing a church or a preacher would want to do is to *liberate* their charges, and the idea of maturity would be a profane and pernicious idea in those circles.

But, secondly, it is perhaps more disturbing to notice in a far 177 larger and more influential and prosperous Christian community a fear of maturity expressing itself in a preaching style that encourages not liberation but immediate dependence. Without going too far into a dangerous field, it is surely possible to be alarmed by the contents of the 1975 hymnal of the Southern

---

*See Elmora Messer Matthews, *Neighbor and Kin,* Vanderbilt University Press, 1965: I quote here especially from chapter 7.

Baptist Convention (whose headquarters are also in Tennessee), and in particular the addiction evinced in that book to what are known in America as 'Gospel Songs'. (These are the evangelical mission hymns which English people associate with the names of Moody and Sankey). To say nothing here about their literary or musical quality — which anyhow are secondary characteristics of hymnody when it is viewed as an indicator of religious culture —the staggering thing about these songs is that whether they are dated 1866 or 1966 they say exactly the same things, using the same vocabulary, showing not the slightest sign of response to those changing needs and insights which have produced new styles in other regions of hymnody. Not every church or member in that Communion takes the anti-educational line that the exclusive use of this kind of folk-song presupposes, but the custom is widespread enough to be alarming.

It is alarming because it goes, as we have said, with certain 178 customs of preaching the Gospel which rely heavily on the generating of instant emotion, and in a sense confine the Gospel as rigidly within a sacred, almost a magical boundary as do the primitives of the valleys; there is a tendency to look for a single stock response (the 'altar call'), to repeat the familiar hortatory incantations, and to discard any attempt to translate the principles of the Gospels into the terms of response to the real pressures under which Christians live in the modern world. A few blanket prohibitions on certain secular habits which are artificially outlawed are enough moral framework for this attenuated Gospel; as for the asking of questions, even the questions are prescribed, and any beyond those are regarded as a sign of unregenerate barbarism which it is the preacher's, or counsellor's duty to change. Exposure to the risk of ecumenical encounter is discouraged. (The Southern Baptist Convention does not seek representation in the World Council of Churches). Indeed, the intensely evangelical approach to religion deals in certainties, safety and precautions against contaminations which run clean counter to the real thrust of the apostolic ministry. It is no answer to this charge to point to the continuing success of the missionary work of such groups, or to the widespread popularity of their preaching. Nor is it an answer to point to the conformity of their members, the unanimity of their resolutions, and the contrasting confusion into which all the other Christians manage to get themselves. The confused liberals are not entitled to make a virtue of their confusions, still less of the failure of mind and nerve which has produced from them so many trivial and sensational judgments during the past two decades; but our contention here is that if one must choose, one is closer to the spirit of the New Testament in leaving the risk of such aberrations open than in making sure, by human means, that they cannot take place. One of Isaac Watt's very few lapses from wisdom (and it was a serious one) was when he paraphrased a line in the Song of Solomon to make the opening line of one of his hymns,

> We are garden walled around,
> a paradise of fruitful ground.

(It is not as if that is how Watts himself lived: he burned his fingers badly at least once by entering into a theological controversy which was, at the time, of nationwide proportions). If we are walled around, the wall is supernatural, not man-made. If we are protected, it is by grace, not by mortal precautions. And if we do try to protect ourselves, we are liable to find ourselves where the rich young ruler stood. It is only a step from confining the Faith exclusively to a single technique, a single form of expression, an unalterable style of song, an untranslatable vocabulary, to confining it to one life-style, one social status, one political outlook: and nobody will argue that this is to interpret faithfully the mind of Christ.

# IX

# *Temptations of Liturgists*

Having already strayed into the field of worship, we must not leave it without considering what is the nature of its aesthetic trajectory. For it is perhaps one error into which protestants have been most liable to fall, to regard preaching as the only important way in which a Christian can receive the Gospel. We must hasten then to say that everything we have said about preaching, and everything we are trying to bring against the artificial style we have just been attacking, can be said of a total act of worship.

In *Words, Music and the Church** I endeavoured to work out one or two of the implications of approaching worship as drama. I did not there deal at all with the substitution of drama for worship, or even say that worship ought to be dramatic: my contention was that worship is, by definition, a kind of drama, and that the only question that need be asked about any specific act of worship was whether it was good drama or bad. I shall not go over that ground again here, but in terms of the present argument I said, and still do say, that it is the object of any act of worship to nourish the 'I', just as much as it is the object specifically of preaching. If a sermon is designed to scatter the congregation each into his or her personal and civic life as a disciple more confident and efficient than each was when they came together to hear it, then this is precisely the purpose of the whole service — to refresh, renew, and revive each person and family present in terms of their own encounter with the Lord.

Now there is no region in which more misconstruction has been placed on the testimonies of the New Testament than here. Historically, it has always been sectarian groups of the ingrown kind who have arrogated to themselves the word 'Primitive', in claiming that because their worship is less structured than that of others they are nearer to the mind of the New Testament. They may be nearer to the practice of the churches of Paul's time —though in many respects such groups usually have not been able to sustain even that modest claim — but there is no evidence at all that they are nearer the mind and vision of the apostles.

There are two places, both in I Corinthians, in which we 182 have reasonably clear evidence of what worship was like in New Testament times, and both are in passages evoked from St. Paul by gross error in the churches he was dealing with. The first is the passage about the Eucharist in I Cor. 11, the second, that about 'speaking with tongues' in I Cor. 14. It is entirely characteristic of our Lord's technique of instruction that he left nothing in the mind of the evangelists upon which they could rely as a specific command in the field of public worship, except only (if it is to be thus interpreted) the words, "Do this in remembrance of me." It is at least questionable whether we can really interpret even those as an instruction that the Church should observe regular Communion services; on the face of it, it is hardly likely that that was the area in which our Lord's mind was moving at that moment. But Paul does give us two very important insights.

I Corinthians 11 : 17-32, the passage from which our tradi- 183 tional 'Words of Institution' come, is Paul's sharp rejoinder to the behaviour of the Christians in Corinth, who had fallen into a curious but, since people are as they are, understandable error. Their meetings must have been (on this evidence) a mixture of conversation over a meal and remembrance of the Lord's Last Supper. They were partly social, partly 'sacred'; or, to put it less awkwardly, they were social occasions with a special intention. They brought their own contributions to the meal and were supposed to share them. There were, in even the large house where it is likely such meetings were held, probably fewer seats than attenders, and some would sit on the floor. It does look as if the more leisured among the congregation would arrive early, with their contributions, claim the best seats, consume their shared meal, and make themselves in every way comfortable before the poorer ones were able to arrive, so that nothing, or only the meagre offerings they could afford, was left for the lower orders, and there was nothing but the floor for them to sit on. This disagreeable intrusion of social privilege into the Christian community naturally causes Paul to issue clear instructions that the food must not be distributed until all who are expected are present, and that there must be no question of reserving comfortable seats for people who can afford to get there early enough to claim them.

Now this does not look like liturgical instruction; but really that is exactly what it is. What has been brought to Paul's notice is nothing that a liturgist could put his finger on and condemn: it is plain bad manners. His instructions include only one point which could possibly be called ceremonious or formal; but that point goes to the heart of the trouble. You must be ceremonious enough, or formal enough, to wait until everybody is there — look at what happens when you don't. So in this very passage which is the keystone of the whole architecture of liturgical custom and study, it is explicitly laid down that liturgy is a function of good behaviour. Who is going to feel refreshed and revived and renewed and more competent as a disciple if there has been that atmosphere in the Christian meeting? 184

The other passage, I Corinthians 14, is built on exactly the same ground, but here it is the speech, not the action, of a Christian meeting that is under discussion. The specific matter is 'speaking with tongues.' Now this faculty is one about which the early Christians were certainly in some difficulty. It was the accepted distinction of certain kinds of prophet, and they were, one gathers, unwilling to extrude it entirely from the place of honour which it had occupied in the religion of their fathers. It had so long been regarded as one of the marks of the possession of that 'spirit' *(ruach)* which was reserved under the Old Covenant for those specially elected by God to carry authority or achieve distinction that it was understandably difficult for Christians to say that the new dispensation needed none of it. In plain fact, the New Dispensation did not need it at all, and Paul here spells out the reason why. But he attacks the problem very gently — and it is worth our while to slow down our pace for a moment and go carefully through what he does say, because it will soon be clear that this is the basic text in the whole Bible on the subject of communication. 185

"I want you," he says, "to prophesy"(v.1). This he says in the first words he writes after putting down that immortal passage about Christian charity, the wholly outgoing, concerned and comprehensive virtue; charity, whose Greek original means 'delight' or 'contentment', and which so clearly here means delight or contentment in other people. Subject to that, says the Apostle, I do indeed want you to prophesy. 186

But once he has used that word, he knows what will be associated with it in the minds of people most of whom think that the only way to prophesy is to speak in tongues. "As to speaking in tongues," he goes on, "you may be speaking to God, but you will 187 not be speaking to each other, since nobody understands you." Clearly implied is: 'And when you are in each other's presence you must not behave as if the others were not there.' Prophecy is something essentially shared, and therefore it must be intelligible. It is interpreting the Lord to the present moment and the present friends. (It is not, here, anything more hierophantic than that). So prophecy will "build up, encourage and console" everybody else present — which is what you are all there to do (v.3).

To put it more starkly: the speaker in tongues 'edifies himself' while the prophet 'edifies the church'(v.4). At once he says (and it is unwise to take the RSV quite literally here*) 'I am content that you all should speak in tongues (sc. 'If you must.'), but it is more important so to communicate that people will understand and benefit' (v.5). This is amplified in the following verses in which Paul emphasizes not only intelligibility but clarity of communication. The famous phrase, 'If the trumpet have an uncertain sound, who will prepare himself for battle' (v.8) is not an instruction to the bugler to blow confidently, but a demonstration of the absurdity of expecting anybody to respond if instead of playing a bugle somebody plays a flute or a harp or a different tune on the trumpet. Good conversation is a matter of signals, and of signals understood by the hearer. All this takes us through vv 6-12. Beyond this, Paul urges people who specialize in speaking with tongues to pray for the gift of communication (or interpretation). Prayer may be offered in a foreign tongue or in the totally incomprehensible sounds of 'speaking with tongues': if it is thus done in public it is useless. Paul's own aim, he says, is to pray, or sing, 'with the spirit and with the mind also.' He remains most anxious not to 'quench the spirit.' If people through their attitude to 'tongues' feel that the communication of Gospel experience is something needing special care and special reverence, this is fair enough; if they think they need special gifts to do it in the presence of others, that too is right. But they must reach for a new kind of

188

---

* It seems clear that *thelo,* the Greek behind 'I would' at this point, or in the RSV 'I want you to', is a word for 'wish' which quickly lost its original positive meaning. Words on which heavy emphasis is customarily laid do not lose, in conversation or writing, their initial letters; but this one did — in classical Greek is it *ethelo*; and most of the time where it appears in the New Testament it is an expression not of a strong wish but more of an expectation or a fairly casual intention. It is perhaps rather like the modern American idiom, 'Do you want to . . .' for 'Please. . . .' (And when all is said, the English future tense is expressed by the use of the word 'will', except in the first person.)

gift. Paul then (v.18) admits that he has done plenty of 'speaking in tongues' in his time, but that he would not dream of doing it in public worship.

Then in his last paragraph he adds something more pro- 189 found. His object is that the church be built up, be allowed to grow, become, in his word, as translated, 'mature.' (v.20). He shows then that 'speaking in tongues' was a manifestation which in Old Testament times did have its effect on the barbarians alongside whom Israel had to live (vv.21-3), but that to use this behavior in the Christian church is a recession towards those days of immaturity. Things are not like that now and we must not behave as though they were. Those were conditions in which superstition was accepted: in which just 'being impressed' was, on the part of the heathen, better than nothing. But we are not content with that kind of thing. Why (v.23), suppose somebody who is a genuine but uninstructed seeker after Christ comes to your meeting: how much use will 'speaking with tongues' be to him? But — again watch the RSV, which is over-reverential here — if this uninstructed person hears prophecy, then he won't be able to miss what you are driving at. He won't just be impressed, or think it was all very marvelous; he will be on his way to conversion.

The ideal meeting, says Paul, is one to which every member 190 has brought something — an experience, an explanation, a song, or whatever it is (oh, well: even a 'tongue', one hears him saying, leaning over backwards not to sound over-severe); and where when you have brought it (v.30) you don't insist on sharing it unless it really will be a help to the community. (If somebody else has stolen your idea, or through what he has said makes it unnecessary for you to speak, you can be silent; and, says anyone who has ever been chairman of any meeting of people, if only a few Christians would learn that, we'd have more time for good works).

Now that quite remarkably comprehensive passage leaves us 191 with exactly the same principle that I Corinthians 11 was based on: good behavior in 'church' is good behavior anywhere. The things that destroy liturgy, on this showing, are at bottom selfishness, lack of interest in people, and a desire personally to shine.

It does not matter how 'primitive' you think you are, how 192 faithful to the New Testament (as so many warring protestant sects used to claim with such stridency in the days of high dispute); if you have not learnt that you have not begun. And while it is no part of my argument to maintain that all ceremonies are superstitious, or on the other hand than everything spontaneous is unprofitable, it is certainly one of my chief contentions that it is against Paul's standard that any liturgical practice, any detail of behavior in worship however apparently minute, must in the end be judged. To that extent I wish to demythologize a good deal of liturgical thought and speech.

Common sense insists that where any group of people are 193 gathered together, there will be a proportion of them who wish to program the rest: to display superior gifts, to shine, to throw dust in the eyes of the rest, to use in-group language which not all understand, to impress by superior articulacy or knowledge; to talk rather than listen, and to feel frustrated if they have not set an insulating space between themselves, or their kind, and their neighbors. Now in analyzing liturgical communications in these terms we must take care not to dismiss people of that kind as being a special or singular menace to the church (or any other society). I for one shall not be lured by all the garrulous, overbearing, boring bad listeners I have ever encountered into a facile communalism that refuses to utter the first person pronoun in liturgy (and that, the way things are going, will soon have us all singing 'When we survey the wondrous cross'). The need of an individual to be himself is not only clamorous; it is part of the machinery God gave him to use and enjoy. We shall be saying that liturgy at its best respects that; but that privacy is one of the many blessings whch turns sour as soon as it is claimed, and remains sweet only when it is conferred.

But still — liturgy is something which people do together: 194 and people in a crowd need some control. It is familiar enough that an uncontrolled crowd can be sinister: that a youngster after a popular football match if he wanders through the city with twenty others may well do things, like breaking shop windows, which he would not do on his own, and very likely would not do were he with his girl-friend. A crowd of people in a church, even if it is forty people in a 400-seater sanctuary, looks to the casual observer so douce and docile that one would hardly attribute to them violent possibilities of that kind. But if their behavior is not controlled they are capable communally (to say nothing of what they do at home) of attitudes and even propositions that do much violence to the principles of the Kingdom. Being in a crowd does not of itself improve people; liturgy is designed to fill that need.

Liturgy is properly and etymologically defined as 'public 195 duty', but in practice it presents itself as a device which makes it possible, profitable and pleasant for people to do things together.

In liturgy, seen as this communal activity that nourishes the community, there is a constant tension between the rights of the individual and his obligations to others, and in due course we shall attend to this (§§209-221). But liturgy is of course describable as a kind of drama. If a tiresome puritan pressure had not given a pejorative sense to the phrase 'play-acting' we would call it that. (I am reminded of C.S. Lewis's audacious but eloquent expression, describing the condition of a man saying the Lord's Prayer as 'dressing up as Christ.') The liturgy — it does not matter how 'informal' or how 'formal' it is, provided it is a settled custom — is something people do together without having to think about it too much; they do it in order that something else may be allowed to happen, and that desired consequence I call the communal, as well as the individual, 'YES!' The 'play' goes to a well-known script; here they rise, there they sit, yonder they move; they say this and that together, they sing together, and at some points they listen. There is nothing surprising, therefore, in the consequence that a satisfactory liturgy must, in its demands, come fairly naturally to the worshipers. If they are attending all the time to *it* the real communication will not have room to come through. Furthermore; the liturgy will be all the more servicable if it implies a discipline — if somewhere in the background there is something against which the unruly will bark its shins. Thirdly, it will be appropriate and efficient if it implies an association between duty and delight; in other words, if it is beautiful.

Taking those three points in order, we are, if we talk about the drama of liturgy, at once faced with the issue of 'participation,' which has become one of the slogans of contemporary liturgical reform. And this in turn obliges us to ask a certain question about the principles of the Reformation. It must be recognized that 'participation' is not in itself a new demand. Aside from any aspects of it which were taken notice of during the Middle Ages, the Reformation itself was, in its treatment of worship, one answer to that demand; but so was that 'Liturgical Movement' which began among European Catholics in the early nineteenth century and of which the Oxford Movement was the first English phase. All those later phases of English liturgical thinking which made special use of the expression 'The People' (like the Parish and People movement of the 1950s, and the publication of books with titles like 'The People's Mass Book') were responses to the same demand, and the very odd use of that expression, 'the People,' has unexpected implications.

The question about the Reformation is: to what extent the demand for participation on the part of 'the people' was a just demand, and to what extent they got what they asked for. Confining ourselves to liturgy, and leaving church politics on one side as far as we can, we find that Luther's reconstitution of the Mass provided a service in which everybody present could, at certain points, vocally join. It was in the vernacular and it had congregational hymns and settings of the singable parts of the service which were congregationally manageable. Since Luther was less of an iconoclast than any of his contemporaries or successors, the Mass as he left it still gave plenty of space to imagination and symbolism. He tried to avoid anything that could not be explained to an intelligent person, and altered only what his theological principles insisted on altering. He made a real effort to distinguish between imagination and superstition, and his gestures were the religious mode of the Renaissance quest for human maturity. Whatever kept Christians *in statu pupillari* he sought to remove. His Preface to the 1526 German Mass is a model of humane consideration for the needs of the educated, and perhaps the best line in it is where he says that if there were ever such a thing as a totally mature Christian he would need no liturgy at all.

And yet — what became of this? Only a generation or two    198
after Luther's death, the Lutheran style had degenerated into a petrified and largely negative protestant ethos, totally unable to stand up to the strains of the Thirty Years' War. After the end of that war (1648) a new evangelical culture, later known as pietism, took the place of the old confessional culture in the minds and affections of most of the active Christians in that communion; Lutheranism in some of the countries outside Germany settled down into the form of a state religion of a kind which has brought all Establishments into disrepute (those statistics, '98% Lutheran' in the Scandinavian countries still appear, to the astonishment of their neighbors).

Or consider the Calvinist strain; Calvin's form of worship in    199
Geneva, we know, was a monumental tribute to the virtues of austerity. The people might participate, true; but only in the singing of metrical psalms. (We cannot give too much significance to the magnificence of the tunes they used for them: that looks like a piece of good luck which Calvin hardly bargained for, and may not have appreciated). Participation there was much more through the understanding, indeed through obedient understanding, of the Scriptures as expounded in the new manner. And in the churches of the Calvinist dynasty — of which the most flexible and responsible must be the Church of Scotland, but in which we

90

must include also the English Congregationalists and their American cousins — it was not long before this exclusively intellectual participation induced a dangerously artificial religion memorably described by the late Edwin Muir in his poem, 'The Incarnate One' as 'The Word made word.' Reactions and rebellions were slow in coming; but the work of the Iona Community in Scotland and of the Church Order Group in England (both begun about the same time, in the 1930s) were both gestures against the 'discarnating' effect of a culture which had begun with a demand for 'the people's' participation and the dethronement of the Pope.

The same has to be said even of the Anabaptist strain — the 200 loosely-knit community of those who went furthest from liturgical principles and from the beginning placed most emphasis on personal experience. Historically the end-product of this has been a free-ranging evangelicalism which has nourished a great number of enthusiastic social reformers and improvers of people's worldly lot, but has always had a fatal tendency to manage other people's religion as well as their temporalities; a little more about this later, but this isn't what people are now calling 'participation.'

One suspects that the root of the failure of the Reformation 201 to do what it hoped to do, and of the paradox that people of protestant principle are now returning with such enthusiasm to ways of worship which only a couple of generations ago would have been dismissed by their grandparents as papistical, is that the greater Reformers failed to notice one thing. This was the extent to which a real response to their overtures depended on literacy. This is less true of Luther than of Calvin. With either of them, however, one can test this thesis by considering how often, if one were engaged in debate about them, one would have to say: 'You misrepresent them: you wouldn't if you had read the Three Treaties of 1520, or the Institutes.' The church orders they generated were founded on massive 'confessions', not infrequently far longer than anything produced in patristic times as an expression of Christian belief and practice. When this exaltation of the written word — in addition to the new emphasis on the written word of Scripture — was allied with a repressiveness as fierce as was that of Calvin's Geneva or Cromwell's England concerning anything that nourished the imagination, a failure of communication was inevitable. Or, in the case of the Anabaptist group, when activism replaced imagination the same consequence followed.

Basically, whatever we may or may not say about the leaders 202 and inceptors of the Reformation, they did fail to communicate exactly what they hoped they would communicate, and it was certainly because of a failure to be relaxed enough about that part of communication we have called the Third Process. Luther understood it but allowed too little for it; I suggest that one would not find a line in Calvin that suggested that he understood it at all.

Hence the renewed demand for participation, most clamorous among the Roman Catholics to whom it came as a new notion after Vatican II, and among the Calvin-based protestants who are now acting as if the Reformation delivered nothing whatever that they needed. For, human nature being what it is, some of these groups are producing people who advocate the abandoning of preaching alongside the reinstatement of liturgy and lectionary; such comical exaggerations are only to be expected when any tradition is put under such strain as that which the Reformation has had to undergo. But if *this* is not 'participation,' what is? 203

Paul in I Corinthians 14:26 said that everybody who came to a Christian meeting brought something with him. (We may possibly imagine that if they brought hymns they may have been very bad hymns; if they brought interpretations, they may have been misinterpretations). It is what people bring with them that geniuses often overlook. You will not get Reformation at all unless there is some commanding and impatient mind behind it; and that mind may overlook something which lesser people will have to take care of. 204

That was the problem for Luther and Calvin, and that is why the Reformation movements are so often like huge dragons whose heads are firmly set in a certain direction, but whose tails swing round and trip up their feet. For if the Reformation protest was against bondage to a church which said, 'You have your liturgy, you have the Latin Bible as we interpret it: you need no more than that, and you can trust us to take care of you,' what in fact happened but that people were now left with the Bible according to Luther, Calvin, Zwingli, or whatever leader they fell under, and with church order according to the Confessions? Was it only the literate who, after all, could be liberated? Was it only those who could responsibly hold a place in a Church Meeting who could be covenanted? Might not all the rest be left in much the same bondage as before — except that in Calvin's case it contained an unconscionable amount of talk and far less beauty than what their fathers had accepted? 205

Participation, according to the classical Reformation, was partial; and the assumption that participation was impossible under the old system of medieval piety was at least only partly 206 true. For we are saying that worship (and every ministry of the Church) is designed to liberate, to evoke the infectious 'YES!' It is inconceivable to think that this was never evoked or achieved for anybody in the Middle Ages. And contemporary opinion about worship is very firmly (perhaps even precipitately) questioning the Reformed principle that it is only words, spoken or written, that will evoke the 'YES!'

If we seem to have strayed rather far from the subject of the 207 drama of liturgy, we can at least now return to it, having established that the peculiar thing about the drama of liturgy is that it needs the setting up of a right proportion between what the participator brings with him and what the Church says to him. In as much as the Reformation was a protest, it was founded in the conviction (very well attested by events spanning the previous two hundred years) that most people were bringing a kind of protest with them; that people, once they were presented with the new deal, would say, 'That is exactly what we wanted to say,' and thank the leading thinkers for saying it. Given that, it would be possible — and it was possible — to communicate something to them which of themselves they could not have conceived. So the Reformation message got through. Naturally it was assisted by purely physical and civic forces. Luther went about it by persuading heads of state; Calvin had the Swiss protests against Vatican pretensions working in his favor. The English Reformers could connect with plenty of unease and alarm in the English generally about the menace of Spain and the political threats presented by a Catholic throne. All that was there in many people for the Reformers to connect with. Was there also, in the same or in other people, a feeling that the Church must no longer keep them in the position of children? Surely there was — going back to the English Lollards (who wanted to read their own Bibles as translated by Wycliffe) and the European dissenting sects upon whom the Establishment bore with so heavy a hand. But when the next stage came, and the new notions were to be presented to the people who had brought that with them, did Luther and Calvin try to present them with more than they could handle? If they did, were they wrong to do so? Those are large questions whose answers must emerge in their own time.

But it does seem that the Reformed demand for 'partici- 208 pation' was both a legitimate demand and at the same time one which it was more difficult to grant in a fruitful and enduring way than the Reformed churches seem to have expected. Perhaps we shall find a key to this paradox by considering the second aspect of liturgy, which is discipline.

Crowd control, or the provision in some way of a convention 209
of good manners, is certainly one of the needs which liturgy has to
meet, and the best way of meeting it is to provide something for
the crowd to do which on the whole it is happy to do. That is the
reason why liturgy is a kind of folk drama, or what has been called
'socio-drama' in recent times. That is, it is a kind of drama in
which the script and the production are far away in the background, and in which all the audience are at the same time players.
It was always this: drama of some kind is part of pagan religion
—whether it is the witch doctors' dance or the plays of Aeschylus
and Euripides. In some forms of liturgy it approaches nearer to
the drama of the proscenium stage, in which the people on one
side mostly watch what is going on the other side, but this is only
an approach; it is never an identity. Liturgy has lost its nature
when it becomes entertainment for a passive audience.

Now consider the discipline laid on liturgy by the existence 210
of an accepted 'script', the 'script' of the Missal or the Prayer
Book. This 'script' is misinterpreted when, in the heat of dispute, it
is regarded as something unwillingly imposed on an audience or a
group of players. It is of no use to any who don't want to join in the
play. Take the very simple, lightweight, graceful 'script' of the
Office of Evensong. This developed from a 'script' originally
devised for a close-knit community, the community of the medieval abbey, where 'scripts' of the kind were provided for regular
worship many times in the day, on the part of people whose daily
labor was carried on right up to the very threshold of the place of
worship. Some were sweeping the cloister and some, a few yards
away, were copying sacred munuscripts, some cooking, some
maintaining the Abbey fabric. The 'script' was a conversation
within the community symbolizing the constant conversation
between human beings and God. The whole conversation was
based on Scripture, and its words, in Latin, were familiar through
generations of use. In a Cathedral or collegiate chapel to-day this
is preserved. It is a happy accident that the very lightness of the
'script' has provided an ideal libretto for what has become a
magnificent treasury of music; but essentially it is chamber-music,
and the place of any worshiper who is not a member of the choir is
that of a listener to a string-quartet.

Discipline and delight seem to meet very closely here, unless 211
somebody finds himself trapped in a Cathedral Evensong and
resentfully complains that it is useless to him because it does not
resemble a revivalist meeting. But — discipline preserves a kind of
equilibrium within which other freedoms can flourish. It has never

been better put than it was put by Canon Joseph Poole, Precentor of Coventry, in the booklet, 'Evensong in Coventry Cathedral' which is provided for worshipers in that place. I am privileged to quote from it here. This is what appears on page 13.

## WHAT IS EVENSONG?

Evensong in Coventry Cathedral is a very tiny fragment of something else: it is a fragment of the worship which is offered to God by christian people, every hour of the twenty-four, in every part of the world. When you come to Evensong here, it is as if you were dropping in on a conversation already in progress — a conversation between God and men which began long before you were born, and will go on long after you are dead. So do not be surprised, or disturbed, if there are some things in the conversation which you do not at once understand.

Evensong is drawn almost entirely from the Bible. Its primary purpose is to proclaim the wonderful works of God in history and in the life and death and resurrection of Jesus Christ. Its secondary purpose is to evoke from the worshiper a response of praise, prayer and obedience.

The English of the Bible is the language that was written and spoken by our ancestors four hundred years ago, when the Bible was first translated into English from the original Greek or Hebrew; it therefore sounds old-fashioned. But its meaning is not out of date.

The service is in three parts.

The first part (which is quite brief) prepares the worshipper for the story which is to follow.

The second part is the narrative of God's redeeming work, beginning in the Old Testament (the Psalms and the First Lesson), proceeding to the New Testament (Magnificat and Nunc Dimittis and the second Lesson) and reaching its climax in the Affirmation of Faith (the Creed).

The third part is man's response to God who has revealed himself in history, in Jesus Christ, and in the Church.

As a description of what Evensong, a wholly 'scripted' act of worship, is supposed to be there is no way of improving on that. (I happen to follow C.S. Lewis in thinking that it is not quite true to say that the language of the King James Bible is that of ordinary people in the early seventeenth century; but certainly its vocabulary is theirs). But notice how that first paragraph gently introduces a certain appropriate attitude to the worshiper and suggests, without saying anything explicit, that he would be wise to adopt it: what is the proper behavior for somebody coming into a room where conversation is going on?

But Canon Poole goes further at two very proper points. 212 Hear this, from the first page of the text of the book (p 5):

When you come in, sit down; relax, be quiet and be still.
Forget the hurry and worry of the world.
For half an hour, or an hour
you are going to be still and quiet
in God's presence.

You may like to use the opportunity for prayer.
On the following pages are some suggestions
to help you to pray.

And at the end (p. 23)

Before you leave

Do not be in a hurry to go; and do nothing
to disturb those who wish to listen to the music
played on the organ.

Kneel or sit for some moments of private prayer.

Thank God for the beauty of the Cathedral: for its music;
and for any particular comfort, or challenge
which your visit has afforded you.

That is all worth study. I have preserved the indentations of the original text. It is written with gentle ceremoniousness, and displayed ceremoniously. The very sight of it slows you down, and helps you to relax. The touch of discipline is applied with such lightness that it is imperceptible. It is all calculated to make the service enjoyable for as many kinds of people as possible including the many who come from very different worshiping traditions, or from none.

Now that is as good an example as I can find of the explicit 213 celebration of discipline which is meant to be delight, in the presence of worshipers to whom its whole tradition may be unfamiliar. (Coventry, after all, is a pretty heathen city, and its

96

Cathedral is still a place of awestruck pilgrimage on the part of many people who never go near a church).

But the most interesting question to ask of anybody or- 214 ganizing worship in any kind of Christian community is — how would you go about producing anything corresponding to that to make your own visitors feel at home?

Well, plenty of people in other kinds of worshiping com- 215 munities are looking for answers. In America especially, it is only a very primitive church indeed now that does not hand the worshiper what is known as a 'Bulletin' (English people would say 'Service paper') when they enter the church. It is now regarded as obligatory at least to show the worshiper some sort of synopsis of what is going to take place. This is commendable, even if, when the paper one gets contains too little help, or the wrong kind, it begins to look like the action of the waitress handing you a menu in the coffee-shop.

I feel sure that it is some kindly impulse towards making the 216 congregation feel at home that produced the following, which appeared (and I am assured that it is not untypical) in a certain Presbyterian church.

Prelude

A Time for Coming Together

Introit

A Time for Drawing near to the Lord, and Praying as he taught us.

Let us Rejoice through music and song. (Hymn specified)

A Time for a Little Humor

Solo

A Time for being sensitive, confessing our hangups, giving thanks to our Lord, and reaching out for each other.

A Time to share the news.

A Time to financially support the work of our Lord.

Solo

A Time to Praise God.

Dedication of our Offering

Scripture Lesson: I Corinthians 15

Let's Sing (Hymn specified)

A Time for Telling it like it is.

(sermon subject specified)

Let's Part with a Song. (your selection)

Benediction

Postlude

If one compares that with, say the Order of Worship for the Lord's Day in the Presbyterian Book of Common Order (USA) or the 1968 *Worshipbook,* one notes differences. The question is whether this is likely to make a stranger feel at home — whether it, with its genial vernacular, its cheerful blue-jeans amiability, does that more effectively than Canon Poole's gentle authority. I do not think the question ought to be closed without careful thought. People who are attracted by the above Bulletin would perhaps think Coventry pompous; but the formula may well be this: are there more people who think Poole pompous than who think the Presbyterian experiment trivial? Are there more specifically of the congregation at (never mind where) who would feel out of place at Coventry Evensong after reading Canon Poole's invitations than there are of those who felt welcomed at Coventry who would also feel quite happy at that other place?

It becomes a question of catholicity. The American church will certainly say, 'This is what we find useful and effective' (I am disregarding any possibility that that Bulletin doesn't represent the broad ethos of that congregation). At Coventry I think they say, 'This really will assist the greatest number of people.' And that represents a different opinion about what the place of the stranger is. In both places you are 'coming in on a conversation.' Is it or is it not true that you are actually left more freedom to make your own contribution to it at Coventry than in the place where you mention your hangups?

Without being too hard on the victims of the 'Bulletin' above quoted, however, it could perhaps be suggested that there is always a danger, when a church sets out to make a friendly approach to those who attend it, that it will try to 'program' what is private to the believer: in this case — what he brings with him to church (following Paul's formula). Where a liturgy presupposes too firmly what kind of people should attend it, and makes too many other people feel out of place because *that* is not what they are bringing to church with them, it offends against our basic formula in attempting to prescribe what it must not prescribe. Of course, no liturgy can entirely avoid such presuppositions, for liturgy operates within the framework of the Faith. But what must always be guarded against is the tendency to narrow the field of acceptance. It could be said that Evensong leaves a wider field than the Bulletin does, and for the following reasons.

What one may presuppose — and therefore should not need to prescribe — in the attender at worship is the Faith itself; as nearly as possible *quod semper, quod ubique, quod ab omnibus*

98

*creditur*, as St Vincent said: what people believe always, everywhere, and with one mind. This in turn takes us back to what we said earlier about tradition in § 44-5: for how much can we be sure that everywhere, always, everybody has held? Are there many things in common between a meeting of Primitive Brethren and the Mass at the Vatican?

Well, there are some things. One is a belief in God, and 220 another, almost universally, is the celebration, in some form, of the Sacrament of the Lord's Supper. If one accepted Unitarians as believers, there is precious little else that one could add; and even then one has to make an exception of the Salvation Army and the Quakers. To that extent, then, liturgy is virtually never a perfect expression of *quod ab omnibus*. But one then has to say that liturgy implies not only belief but also custom; and variety of custom digs deep trenches between different traditions. So there is never a Christian service at which everybody feels at home equally. The testimony of Scripture, in insisting that we never omit eschatology from our thinking on such matters, insists that this is what we must expect. Therefore it is always false to speak of perfection in such concerns, although it is equally wrong to disbelieve in its existence. The fact that the only perfect worship is 'the Marriage Supper of the Lamb' does not dispense us from the duty of making right decisions in those concerns to which our membership of the Church Militant calls us.

It is, then, a question of discerning how near we can get, 221 or how many avoidable mistakes we can avoid. Now the most tractable problem we can wrestle with is, how worship should communicate. If our basic principle is right, that its object is the liberation of the worshiper, what disciplines does this suggest as right, and which does it demand that we avoid?

# X
# *Relaxing Into Beauty*

The question posed at the end of the last chapter can be   222
answered only by bringing in the third category under which we
promised to discuss liturgy: that of beauty. This can be discussed
only in the light of that discipline with which we have been
dealing, because to discuss it without relating it to reason will be to
invite sentimentality. We shall approach it by considering certain
primary components of public worship beginning with public
prayer.

Public prayer is the part of worship which appeals least to the   223
sceptic, and about which many honest people can be persuaded,
given sufficient sense of freedom in expressing themselves, to
voice doubts. Such people find it relatively easy to believe in
private prayer, which they usually hold to be some sort of conversation with God, consisting very largely of petitions. What usually
happens is that any persuasive teaching about public prayer that
they can be induced to accept reveals a need of reconstructing the
ideas they had about private prayer.

But our question is, in what sense does a worshiper partic-   224
ipate in public prayer? It is over-simple to say that if the prayer is
so set out that he can join in either the whole of it or responses to it,
it will give him a better chance of participation than if it is said
wholly for him by a priest. The question in the mind of the seeker
after the truth of this matter is, 'Am I *really* praying?" And in these
days of liturgical experiment and reconstruction, few of us
involved in it have escaped the experience of hearing the very
people who doubted the propriety of 'free prayer' by the minister
or liturgical prayer by the priest say that now that they have to
read it all out of a book, in language that is strange to them, they
are no better off; indeed, they are worse off because they are so
busy finding the right place or remembering not to say 'Glory be to
God in high', but 'Glory to God in the highest' that their minds
have no leisure to pray. Those who speak so speak rightly and

74133

discerningly. They need *space,* they need room to pray; being to this extent 'programmed' by liturgists they find exasperating: it is the same whether they are accustomed to a liturgy that has been changed, or whether they are not accustomed to one and are now faced with one.

That sufficiently disposes of the idea that to keep the congregation talking is to keep them participating. The truth is that whatever their tradition, Christian groups are nourished when the 'script' of the drama is sufficiently in the background for them not to have consciously to attend to it. New or contrived liturgies produce an experience as different from what they obscurely but rightly think of as worship as reading a play around the room is different from being in the theatre and acting it. 225

Everybody really knows — it makes no difference what their tradition is — that in worship they need space to contemplate and meditate. Perhaps the opinion that the constant attending of services where the liturgy is wholly prescribed is a superstitious use of 'vain repetition' is now dying; it must be, if so many formerly unliturgical communions are making such a point of issuing directories of worship. But it always was an error to think that way — it was, I am afraid, an error even when the Puritans said it, though in their case perhaps forgiveable. 226

Now both the tradition of free prayer and that of liturgical prayer really, at their best, admit this. But the real difference between those traditions, when they are seen (as they used to be but are not now) as quite distinct, is that if you believe in free prayer — that is prayer in public which is unpredictable to the congregation whether it is composed on the spur of the moment or written down beforehand — you believe that the Church is a family. This is what the classic puritans believed; and they also had specific ideas about what a family was. To say the church is a family is to say that this worshiping community is a group of people who know each other well, who are personally 'covenanted together', in the great puritan phrase, to follow and serve the Lord, and that in such a group there are plenty of things that each can presuppose about his neighbor. Not, in the best puritan circles, that you (the minister or other ordinary leader of worship) prescribed what people brought with them: you were able to assume it, just as the ordinaries of the anglican services could. Why, in the 'vintage' puritan churches it was even assumed that a minister, once ordained to a congregation, (he might well be somebody who grew up in it) would remain with them all his life. For various reasons even in those days he might not; he might, for 227 one thing, be put in prison for nonconformity, or forbidden to exercise his ministry; or he might, like John Owen, be made Vice-Chancellor of Oxford University; but the Savoy Declaration makes no provisions for the kind of ministerial movement from one parish to another that is now common in all denominations.

In other words: that which is spontaneous is local. The  228
church is the family writ large, the minister the father of the family. Now in such circles, although it looks as if the minister's prayers (conceived or extemporary) will be totally unpredictable to his congregation, that is not the case. For one thing, they would in fact take much the same form week by week; for another, they were, in the classic days, full of allusions to and quotations from Scripture (in Scotland, from the metrical psalms also). For a third, the rapport between people and minister was very close. The puritan suspicion of ceremonies may be judged now of historical interest only; but it will not do to accuse them of lack of sympathy with their people in their insistence on 'free prayer.'

It is perfectly clear that the modern interest in liturgical forms  229
on the part of the heirs of puritan traditions is the product of modern social conditions. If a church is no longer a family, if people now always move from place to place (and ministers as well), if no church expects to bury the same people they once baptized, the 'family' image breaks down — and indeed where people try to preserve it it survives only in a rather oppressive kind of possessiveness — the lamentation that 'all our young people leave us', or the tiresome insistence that only people who have been in the same church for twenty years or so qualify for a call to eldership. What has happened is simply the removal of that assurance that you knew what people were bringing with them that supplied in the 'free' worship of other days what the removal of liturgy had taken away.

What the old tradition of free prayer had in common with the  230
liturgies it replaced was, of course, the leaving of space for the individual worshiper's contemplation. It was not that he *attended* to the free prayer with any more assiduity than that with which his neighbor *attended* to the anglican liturgy. The prayer sparked off his own prayers. The Scriptural language and quotations provided the same sense of security, the same definable field in which his own thoughts could move about, as did Cranmer's English in the prayer book.

In fact, in the best days, both had a respect for public  231
language. And we can now say that one of the primary necessities in any public prayer is a sense of public language. Public language

is that which will be understood by the greatest number of people; private language is the in-group language of a closed community. Public language embraces; private language excludes. (see § 216 for an example). The public language of the Church is public to the Church even if it sounds 'private' to those outside it. The 'of the Church' from which it is primarily derived is the Bible; therefore in those days when only one translation of the Bible was in use, this was the natural source of the Church's speech: and it is equally present in the free prayer of a puritan divine and in Cranmer's Prayer Book.

But of public language we can say two things: one always, the 232 other in certain circumstances. The first is that it is subject in the widest sense to the discipline of reason. This is offended against whenever language is used loosely, or in a private or sectional way. Therefore in liturgical language of any kind elementary grammatical or syntactical errors are not only out of place but damaging. One of the results of the present confusion of social values is a very widespread neglect of this principle. One recalls how puzzled children in a school are when told that TONITE is the wrong way to write 'to-night,' when they constantly see it so written in public advertisements on the street or on television. The Bulletin we quoted contains a split infinitive at the one point where its writer attempts to form a sentence; the fact that this usage is becoming so common in America as to be virtually accepted (and that a well known dictionary of American usage classes its avoidance with unnecessary pedantries) may be a comment on the slipping of social values but it does not justify its use in public speech. Public language is always precise and graceful, simply because it will thus communicate with the largest number of people. It observes rigid conventions and standards which might well be inappropriate to private speech. When great matters are at stake, as in the law courts or in Parliament, procedures rigidly adhered to include the use of language.

But public language may also be beautiful. It is not always so. 233 It is not so, one has to admit, in the kind of legal document which aims only at imparting reliable information (see § 27 above). But a legal document never expects the answer 'YES!' It is, precisely, when public language gets that answer that we call it beautiful. The quality of beauty is what evokes that answer.

So we here pick up the point we made in § 143 about a specific 234 Cranmer prayer: that its acknowledged beauty, a tiny example of that quality which we attribute to the whole Prayer Book, is not a quality that its translator sought. It is something we attribute to it;

it is what makes it memorable and friendly and august. But Cranmer was translating, not consciously creating beauty; he was concerned with reason and duty much more than with making an effect. But it would be possible to attribute the same quality to the conceived or spontaneous prayer of a divine in the puritan tradition, speaking with his 'family.' It would probably be calamitous if he were at pains to make it beautiful (one remembers W.R. Maltby's indignant protest at the 'blasphemy' of 'eloquent prayer'); but there is no more reason to deny it beauty than to say that a Cathedral can be beautiful and a puritan meeting house can never be.

If reason informs the Church's speech, and if its purpose is the liberation of hearers, then beauty will come. No legal document liberates; but poetry always does. Similarly we have already said that the beauty we attribute to the King James Version was not sought by its translators.* 235

But we have also said that beauty, or anyhow the work of the artist, is exactly what gives space for the liberation of the perceiver's thought and affections. That which is beautiful — that which is perceived as such by many generations and virtually every kind of people — is that which opens and sensitizes the faculties of memory and apprehension. It evokes a welcome. And the curious thing about it is that while it will not do that if it is obscured by neglect of reason, neither will it do it if it is obscured by too much anxiety for explicit and immediate understanding. 236

One of the things which people used to a very familiar liturgy — to which they don't have to *attend* in a stressful fashion — often say is that each time they hear it, a different word makes a special impact. In the course of a whole service it may be one word that evokes a small 'YES!' — but that is enough. It may not happen, but it happens often enough to make it worth while to be there constantly. But another related quality of the best public liturgy is that it leaves a certain right to explicitness unclaimed. 237

We justify the use of 'the best' in that last sentence as follows. Consider a prayer of Confession, in which a congregation corporately admits in God's presence all those decisions which have obscured the purpose of God in each. Broadly, one can think of 238

* A beauty, we might say, not totally unflawed. 'The desolations of many generations', Isa. 61:4, is a bad slip from euphony, and the very odd breaches of syntax in St. John 17, 'I pray. . . that they might. . .' have misled many an aspirer after sacred sounds into neglect of the rules of sequence of tenses.

three ways of composing such a prayer for public use. One way is to use the General Confession in the old Prayer Book, in which what we have to say about ourselves specifically is that 'we have left undone those things which we ought to have done, and we have done those things which we ought not to have done.' The statement is introduced by a reference to the straying sheep in Isaiah 53, and followed by the summary, 'and there is no health in us' (a proposition which the raised eyebrow of modernism often omits when the prayer is transcribed elsewhere). A second form is the General Confession in the alternative liturgy suggested by the puritan party (probably written by Richard Baxter) at the Savoy Colloquy of 1661, in which the specification of actual errors is no more explicit, but the whole condition of general sin is eloquently and exhaustively attested by abundant Scriptural references. A third fashion is this:

> Almighty God: you love us, but we have not loved you; you call, but we have not listened. We walk away from neighbors in need, wrapped up in our own concerns. We have gone along with evil, with prejudice, warfare and greed. God our Father, help us to face up to ourselves, so that, as you move toward us in mercy, we may repent, turn to you, and receive forgiveness; through Jesus Christ our Lord. Amen.

That is from the Service for the Lord's Day in the *Worshipbook* (1968, 1972) of the American Presbyterian Churches. The most iconoclastic of puritans could not well accuse it of being beautiful: its language is loose, its rhythm bumpy, and its teaching that the object of confession is to face up to ourselves is at best doubtful. But it must also be said that it does not do its work. Its greatest error is in descending suddenly to the specific. The sins it invites us to confess are all social: neglect of the needy, prejudice, warfare, greed, and (whatever in this context it is supposed to mean) 'evil'. So the worshiper's reaction is naturally to check whether those particular errors have appeared in his conduct during the past week, and if not, to dissociate himself from the whole process. Or at least — I should claim that that is what his attitude should be. To confess that you have walked away from a needy neighbor when you are unconscious of having done so, or when you have actually done the reverse of that during the past week, is an offence against the truth. And to claim that if you haven't done it, somebody else has, and you must confess his sins as well as yours, is a very dangerous precedent indeed, and is, I think, an example of what I believe to be a misconception in that book of worship

106

concerning the relation between 'I' and 'We' in worship (see below, § 349). What provision, one may ask, is made here for the sins of sloth and pride? What provision for bent philanthropy? For corrupt motives? For bad temper and impatience and the preference of remote and impalpable obligations over undramatic, demanding and very close obligations? How easily this prayer would come to the character in the *Screwtape Letters* who prayed that God would heal his mother's bad temper but not her rheumatism, or the other in a different place in the same author's teaching who was at church when he ought to have been washing the dishes. I am reminded of the irreverent comment of a young man — who later himself became a distinguished divine — about a somewhat expansive benediction offered by his father from a nonconformist pulpit in some such words as these:

And now
may the blessing of God Almighty, the Father, the Son and
    the Holy Spirit
be upon us all
and upon all people everywhere,
near and far
black and white
rich and poor
    (and so on, no doubt)
now and evermore.

'Just like the Old Man', said the son, 'to leave out the Chinese.'

When we are specific, it is the gaps that at once appear. It is 239 the same principle as the need to mention everybody's birthday if you mention one person's, to panegyrize every dead member if you panegyrize one.

So we come to the place of understanding in worship — a 240 problem which the Reformation raised, which in the English tradition the puritans interpreted, and which now has everybody by the ears. That which is unintelligible is manifestly unprofitable — as 1 Corithians 14 said. But does intelligibility, as an aid to maturity and liberation, always mean total explicitness? It cannot — you can prove it by (if you are not a lawyer) trying to make sense of a complicated legal trust. Total explicitness uses the techniques and delivers the results appropriate to the telephone directory (§§ 27-8). Total explicitness would enslave if it carried the least weight of obligation. (None of us would be pleased to be required to know the telephone directory by heart, or to have passages of it read to us daily). Even partial explicitness can, as we have just seen, be dangerous. In public prayer it is especially so because it invites the worshiper to argue with the composer of the prayer, and thus distracts him from the purpose of making contact with God. In other words, there is no way of opting out of the implications of the old General Confession: there are plenty of ways of by-passing the modern one, and if by any chance any sectional prejudice on the part of the author of the prayer communicates itself to the worshiper (even if I am being unjust in this judgment about that prayer, the risk is there), then the communication between the believer and God has gone, because the prevenient liberation has been frustrated.

And yet — so complex is this matter — there seems to be a 241 kind of explicitness which does not fall under this condemnation. Is there not something in liturgical language which could correspond to the evocative and beautiful effect of Milton's use of proper names in *Paradise Lost* or Watts's Pisgah and 'old Canaan' in his delectable hymn, 'There is a land of pure delight'?

Normal opinion and experience suggest that there is a place 242 for specificity in intercession and in thanksgiving. In some groups when general intercessions are made, persons for whom intercession is especially desired are named; or when thanksgivings are made, occasions of special personal thanksgiving are mentioned. This is done either in the form of a 'bidding' ('You are especially asked to pray for. . . . .') or by arranging a pause in the course of a prayer in which members of the congregation mention their private intentions of intercession or thanksgiving. The revised American Episcopal Prayer Book, for example, provides for this second course. And, of course, a personal reference is always regarded as in order in any service specially designed for remembrance. How is this different from the particularity we objected to in Confession?

The difference is formal. It is a matter of interceding 'for all 243 who are in need, and *especially*. . .' or of giving thanks 'for all blessings, *and especially*. . .' — the focusing of a general prayer for a moment on some particular point. The difference is also in content: that of which we are personally ashamed we are properly reticent about: that of which we are proud (sympathy, rejoicing) we want to share. The idea of saying 'Let us confess our sins remembering *especially*. . .' is so indecent as to be inconceivable even on the part of the most wayward modern liturgists. If we confess our inextricable involvement in Original Sin, that is as communal as we can properly get. But in intercession it will not be enough if we are *merely* specific; prayer for this or that person about whom we are concerned, shared with the Christian community, can be gracious. Intercession that always mentions certain specific general needs and always leaves others unmentioned is as bad as partially specific confession. Thanksgiving for certain specified blessings and omission always of others is again dangerous. In either case the result will be that those whose prayers are never offered through the prayers of the leader will be moved to argue with him, or to feel resentful at being always left out. And since it is impossible to pray for *all* kinds of blessing, or *all* kinds of need, common prayer is at its best when it is most comprehensive, and briefest.

But none of this means that the imaginative invasion of the 244 specific into prayer on specific occasions is always tasteless. I recall that when the then Minister of St Giles' Cathedral, Edinburgh, in an invocation of blessing upon the Edinburgh Festival, prayed for blessing on, among other artists, 'those who make us laugh', the national newspapers gave it a headline. Well they might: that is not a subject often on the lips of divines of the Kirk in their public ministries — but nobody could fail to be conscious of a new dimension of reality in public prayer at the moment when that was said. Or again, quoting once more from those archives of Coventry Cathedral which contain so many liturgical delights, consider this prayer conceived by the Precentor for a service commending into the Almighty Hands the perplexing and at the time alarming prospect of British unity with Europe:

> Come, Father and Lord, creator of this beautiful and hospitable world,
> Come, Lord Jesus Christ, the light which the darkness has never mastered, and never will,
> Come, Holy Spirit, Lord and life-giver,
> Come, Lord, come:

> Accept the tribute which we pray
> of gratitude for the graces and beauties of Europe,
> of sorrow for the follies and cries of Europe,
> of reverance for the sanctities of Europe:

> Come, puissant Lord,
> refresh us with the riches of thy creation,
> Come, benign Redeemer,
> rescue us from the misuse of thy creation,
> Come, Holy Spirit, the only Ruler of our unruly appetites and affections,
> dispose us to share the resources of thy creation.
> Come, Lord, come.

Create among the nation of Europe
   justice
   and comity,
   and joy;
   for now all things sigh to be renewed,
   and only in thy will is our peace;
   who reignest God
   today
   tomorrow,
   always.
      Amen.

That masterpiece repays study by any liturgist. It is indeed topical: it does reach out to what anybody coming to that service would bring with him — which was chiefly a sort of shaky hope that this massive political adjustment would be made without disaster. It was the combination of piercing particularity with a general ambience of assurance in the presence of mysteries far greater than those which at that moment puzzled everybody that made that a great example of the prayer-writer's art. And I think it has exposed, as clearly as we can hope to see it, the sensitive secret of this high responsibility of liturgy-making. It is, of course, the secret of how to behave in that area of communication in which we have already so often said that certain decisions must not be made. This will have aroused prayer in the worshipers; this will have opened a field of liberated prayer because in its reaching out it showed a reticent respect. It sought out the worshiper at his best — the great thing the worshiper was waiting to say. In a prayer of confession you are not required to seek out the worshiper's sin (Matthew 7:1 is sufficient authority); in such a prayer as this you are enabled to seek out that which in him is struggling — and on that particular occasion was struggling painfully — for expression.

And when you have done that, beauty will follow as the night 245 the day, for you are an artist. Now this is no doubt the place to say that considerations of this kind are of much more importance than questions such as whether we should avoid archaic language. Upon this matter we can now fairly easily see our way. It is important that the language shall be exact, that words be used as precision tools; it matters not at all whether those tools were made yesterday or four hundred years ago.

There is no reason why we should any longer have patience 246 with people who claim that only contemporary language is fit for worship. What is needed is precision plus those devices of art which give words wings. Nobody wants imprecise or misleading words to try and fly. It is one of the constant astonishments to any who know and value Cranmer's Prayer-Book that so few actual words in it have so changed their meaning or passed out of use as to demand retranslation or replacement. 'Vouchsafe' is certainly one, 'eschew' is probably another, and 'prevent' in the sense of 'Go before' is a third. Are there as many as three more? Yes — 'curates' for 'clergy' must go. And Cranmer had a less sure touch when translating lyrics (his *Veni Creator* is plodding stuff), so perhaps his *Te Deum* needs looking at.* 'Thou didst not abhor the Virgin's womb' is an expression which I would support the opinion of Percy Dearmer, given fifty years ago, in regretting (and, like him, I wish it had not been preserved in 'O come, all ye faithful'); 'abhor' is now the wrong word; 'disdain' is what it means. But really —how far one has to go to find even those few examples. The language of the Prayer Book presents far fewer surface-difficulties than that of the King James Bible.

It would be different had it been less ably translated; so much 247 is obvious. It would have been different, for example, if its language had been on the literary level of the Scottish Metrical Psalms (which are revered in an almost tribal fashion by the Scots, but hardly twenty lines of which are tolerable as literature). No: it cannot be maintained that the Prayer Book is imprecise, or that it fails to communicate. What is maintained is that its cadences evoke the manners of an age which has passed away — and the desirability of that is a much more debatable proposition.

But I should not have quoted from the Precentor of Coventry 248 if I thought that people should not attempt to write modern prayers, or that when they do, they always fail to do as well as the Prayer Book does. That I do not at all believe. If anyone wants further evidence that it can be done by real artists, to the edification of everybody, let him turn either, for modern material in the grand style, to the work of Eric Milner-White (the most familiar of whose prayers is that now so widely associated with the Service of Nine Lessons and Carols at Christmas), or, for the use of an openly contemporary style *Contemporary Prayers for Public*

---

* I happen to think Alan Luff's stress-meter translation of this easily the best and most singable version available. It can be found at #100 in *Hymns and Songs* (1969) and #21 in *Ecumenical Praise* (1976)

*Worship*, (1967), *More Contemporary Prayers* (1972) and *Contemporary Prayers for Church and School* (1976). All edited by Caryl Micklem.

The question brought up by these and others of the same kind, whether it is proper nowadays to address God in public prayer with the 'you' pronoun, is not, compared with other questions we have been examining, important. In the days of Cranmer and of the King James Version, 'thou' had not disappeared from ordinary speech, and therefore when those versions were set down it did not have quite the remote effect that it has now. There is, we must say, nothing wrong with remoteness of that kind; but for my part I am unable to discourage 'you' provided that it is used as precisely, and that the English of which it is a part is as good, as we have found in the older versions.* As the editor of *Contemporary Prayers for Public Worship* said in his preface, the use of the new form has the effect not merely of translating traditional thoughts into a modern form of speech, but of generating new thoughts. That is true: the medium, we remember, is at least part of the message. And therefore, if the use of 'you' liberates new thoughts, perhaps it will also make it less easy for certain older thoughts to find expression. In particular the classic Collect form of opening, 'Almighty God, who. . . .' translates so awkwardly in nine cases out of ten that you find you have, not to rewrite the old prayer, but to write a new one. This seems to put a good case for the retention of both forms in worship, which in practice produces a sense of incongruity which is almost imperceptible, and far less damaging than any hectic or exclusive modernism. It also makes it possible to say that the fashion of rewriting hymns of the older kind so that they too speak in the 'you' language is mostly a waste of ingenuity. The demands of rhyme and meter are usually so great as to make awkwardness in the new versions inescapable. Here again, one tends to say that a hymn written nowadays will probably sound most natural and communicate best if it is written in 'you', and allows the fresh thoughts that this form of address generates to run free, while it really does nobody any harm to sing in the same

---

* I am indeed prepared to testify that it was the sight of the manuscript of *Contemporary Prayers for Public Worship*, sent to me by the publisher for assessment, which persuaded me that in my own work along this line I must renounce 'thou' for ever.

service 'Father, unto thee we raise this, our sacrifice of praise.'*

Enough of these important but secondary concerns. In devis- 250 ing public prayer and liturgy, it is the principle of I Corinthians 14 that counts for most — the reaching out for what is best in the worshiper, and expression of this. The effect of such devotions is bound to be the liberation, the growth, the movement towards maturity of the worshiper and of the Church.

---

* The subject is not important enough to require hard and fast rules. One senior contemporary writer has gracefully permitted the rewriting, in 'you', of a hymn which he wrote in 'thou' and which was first published in 1950: for which see *Hymns for Celebration* #23 and *Westminster Praise* #41, comparing both with *Hymns Ancient and Modern*, 422; and Donald Hughes's superb hymn. 'Creator of the earth and skies' (in 'thou' in *Hymns for Church & School*, 1964, #287) certainly becomes more trenchant in 'you', (*Westminster Praise*, #57) which before his death he personally authorized).

# XI
# "*The Way To Heaven's Door*"

Sweetest of sweets, I thank you: when displeasure
did through my bodie wound my minde,
you took me thence, and in your house of pleasure
a daintie lodging me assign'd.

Now I in you without a bodie move,
rising and falling with your wings:
we both together sweetly live and love,
yet say sometimes, *God help poore Kings.*

Comfort, 'lle die; for if you poste from me,
sure I shall do so, and much more:
but if I travell in your companie
you know the way to heaven's door.

George Herbert

Enough has already been said about preaching and the use of  251
Scripture in liturgy to make it unnecessary to add here more than
a note or two in the light of our more recent arguments. Preaching
is the bringing into the present of what Scripture has to say to each
age, each congregation at each moment. In it the preacher must
celebrate and use the gifts of his own 'I'; what he says must be the
product of his own "YES!" And in that reaching out towards the
best in his hearers he will so extinguish the 'I' as to be entirely
taken up with the duty of arousing the "I" and the "YES!" in each
of his hearers. And their participation will be in their scattering
each to his duty. We have certainly said enough to dispose of any
trivial arguments about the outdatedness or irrelevance of the
monologue sermon. If it is not grounded in that Scripture which
the hearer has "brought with him", and does not reach out
towards that life which he is bringing with him, it will fail. If it is
not what only *that* preacher could say at *that* moment, it will die
before it is born.

And concerning the public reading of Scripture we have also    252
had something to say (§§49-50); we can simply here take up the
point we made about liturgical lectionaries by noting that they
really depend for their effectiveness on the assumption that the
hearer is indeed "bringing scripture with him" to church. Whatever will make him free of the Scriptures, and give him greater
delight and profit in reading them for himself, the church must in
some way provide. Only one more point will have to be made
about this in a later section. As for the use of modern translations:
this is unexceptionable when the translations have enough weight
to carry them across the gap between the reader and the hearer.
Some, as is well known, read better in public assembly than
others. The fault of the often brilliant J.B. Phillips translation is in
its occasional garrulousness — he is a master of the epigram and
the telling phrase, but he does not preserve the condensed energy
of the older versions, or of the Revised Standard Version. The
New English Bible is sometimes excellent (when it is a passage that
needs reading swiftly), but in passages which need ceremonious
treatment it usually lets us down. The Jerusalem Bible is, again,
often very rhythmical and ceremonious, but it is capable of such
bathos as 'Peter was upset' in John 21: 17, which is a very nasty
moment. Immediate intelligibility is sometimes delusive: some
uses of modern translations cause some hearers to find the meaning less clear (§54 above); others cause others to think they have
understood what they have not understood. But all this is very
much a matter for local judgment guided by the principles we are
here suggesting.

But what of church music? Well, this is the point at which    253
what one might call a fully fledged and recognized professional
discipline collides head-on with the needs of the sacred liturgy. We
thought it necessary to remind the reader that preaching is an art
form, and that liturgy is a sort of drama; but there is no question
about music. The results of this have been in the mostly very
fruitful and friendly controversy (occasionally, human nature
being what it is, erupting into rancour) between the musicians and
the ordinaries of worship.

Not to repeat too tediously what I (and others better) have    254
written elsewhere about the use, functions and forms of church
music, we are here content to say that broadly speaking music in
church is either folk song or professional music, and has been so
throughout most of the church's life. There is music which unmusical people can join in — which is some form of hymnody; and
there is music which the same people do not join in, but which is

made in their presence and for their edification. There is no music in church which can be approached simply as concert music, because at a concert everybody is musical (everybody had brought a considerable store of music 'with him') while in church not everybody has any appreciation of music at all.

If then the purpose of the music, whatever its form or style, is 255 the same liberation which is the purpose of everything else in the liturgy, what limitations does this impose, and what fruitful disciplines does it offer?

Begin with the most familiar and now universal kind of 256 church music, which is hymnody. Hymns can be described in many ways. They are the shanties or work-songs of the Christian work-force. They are lyric expressions of Christian conviction and experience. They are (especially in those Reformed circles where their modern form had its origin) the congregation's response to acts of worship done on their behalf. Above all, they are the classic example of the demand for congregational "participation" fully stated and granted. Congregational hymnody as part of the liturgy had no place at all in medieval Catholic worship; it is strictly a product of the Reformation — which since 1964 has been fully recognized and espoused by Catholics as well as Protestants.

The actual use of hymns, and people's approach to them, 257 must be governed by the kind of liturgical life into which they are introduced. Communities which have a prescribed liturgy regard them as an adornment (some members of such communities regard them as an intrusion). Those in which liturgy was less 'conversational' in form, and more heavily reliant on the kind of communication which had to be set up between a leader of worship who says everything and a congregation which participates silently, found in hymns a welcome occasion for the congregation's actually giving expression to what they had "brought with them". It was soon found that metrical psalms, which throughout the Calvinist tradition had been the only lawful form of congregational song, were insufficient to express the convictions of Christians, and from this defective condition Isaac Watts delivered the English-speaking Calvinists in the early years of the eighteenth century. But distinctions of this kind in practice usually escape the worshiper, who finds in hymns (there are very few exceptions to this) the friendliest and most easily-remembered formulae for the expression of his personal faith.

John Julian in 1892 estimated that there were 400,000 hymns 258 in existence in English. The number nearly a century later must be much higher. This is an indication of the fact that hymns are

117

expressions of the Church's faith which are not unchanging, as are the classic Creeds and the Scriptures, but which express it in response to the pressures of changing custom and mode of apprehension. They are, liturgically, an extension of the 'propers' of the Mass — those prayers which change from season to season and week to week as distinguished from those which remain constant. But hymns change not only from service to service but from age to age.

Our concern here is not with their history or nature, but with the decisions which have to be taken about them. If there are half a million hymns in English, those decisions are clearly complex. They are taken at different levels by writers and composers, by editors of hymnals, by those who select them for services, and by those who direct their performance.   259

Hymnody combines the arts of lyric poetry and of music, and the practitioners of both have to form their composition in a 'folk' style. (I do not of course use that expression in any of its modern technical senses.) This means that the writer of a hymn and the composer of its tune are reaching out for the best that is in an uncultivated singer.   260

Hymn text-writing is a difficult art — as any who have had to read through the efforts of those who enter for hymn-writing competitions have learned the hard way.* Whether in words or in music, no hymn will get off the ground unless its author is primarily 'reaching out' to the people he hopes will sing him. On the whole, the defect in text writers nowadays is to provide something which people already have, written less well than it was written by the author who provided it before. Isaac Watts and Charles Wesley, who dominated the hymnody of the eighteenth century, were in a favored position; people were reaching out for anything they could provide because nobody else was providing it. The twentieth century writer has to ask whether what he is offering is what only he, and only his age, could offer, and whether it either says better what had been said before, or says what has not been said before. His task is not hopeless — as far as I can see it never   261

---

* On the whole, such events should be discouraged; winning a prize in a competition is a rather different (and inferior) motive from that which we are hoping for in a hymn writer. Should anyone be in doubt of this, I urge him to find, if he can, a copy of *National Hymns,* by Richard Grant White, published in New York in 1861. Here, in the funniest book on hymnology I have ever found, the author rehearses and analyzes the entries for a competition held at that time to encourage new hymnody for the heartening of the nation during the Civil War.

will be — because there are always new things to say, new emphases to be celebrated, and new lights to be discerned from Scripture —which, one hopes it is unnecessary to say, should be the starting point for all hymnody. But contemporary hymnody at its best celebrates that alertness for what the unliterary or unmusical are waiting to say which is exactly the quality one wishes to see in those who take any liturgical decision. Frederick Pratt Green, Brian Wren, and Fred Kaan are excellent examples from British hymnody of the application of this technique, as are Martin Franzmann and Bradford G. Webster in the USA (not to mention those three great writers of the earlier generation, Walter Russell Bowie, Howard Chandler Robbins and Francis Bland Tucker). Text writing stays fresh when writers are critical both of the established cliché and of the awkward and affected modern idiom: the cliché will dull the apprehension of the singers, the clumsy or overbearing cast of language will irritate them, and in either case the communication will be frustrated because the singer will not be able to say, 'That's what I was waiting to say.'

In the music of hymns we find the same principle. It is always, 262 however, important to recognize the special problem of 'music for the unmusical'. It is well known that people are much readier to sing words that are rubbish to a good tune, than a tune which is rubbish to good words. They can read, and the art of the hymn writer, even when misapplied, translates theological technicality into images that carry it into the theologically untrained mind. Nobody can do this for music; and music, especially when uncritically accepted by the unmusical, becomes often the more memorable part of the hymn, and gives tawdry, ill-written or positively misleading words a passport to the singer's affection. For this reason, though the appeal of music must be recognized, it must to some extent be controlled. We know what popular songs can do for pernicious political movements. Just because people are singing they are not necessarily singing their way to faith.

It is here, and especially at the musical level, that decisions 263 have to be taken by the composer, the chooser of hymns, and the performers and interpreters of them. And if we watch the composer for a moment we find him exposing, perhaps more fully than any of the other characters in our story, what the principle of communication really is. For in writing music that unmusical people are to sing, he restricts his art to that which will reach out and touch what the singer is 'bringing with him', but he then exercises his art in order to reach out and touch what is best in what the singer has brought. There are various forms of hymnody which are very clearly composed by people who are able enough musicians, but who are incapable of reaching out far enough or sensitively enough to connect with the singer at all. What such musicians produce is often good choral music, and not infrequently music which the singer would profit by hearing, but it tends not to become successful hymnody because the singer does not feel that the music is inviting people like him to join in. Editors who have a special passion for pedagogy compose, encourage, or commission music of this kind; and to the extent that their approach to their work is inspired by a pedagogy that is snobbish rather than compassionate or respectful towards the taught, the music will be inaccessible and vexatious — good perhaps for some purposes, but not for that for which it was designed.

On the other hand, hymnody can be composed or commis- 264 sioned or encouraged which deliberately aims below the best that the worshiper can bring. This is the basis of my criticism of the Baptist hymnody I referred to in §177, but it evokes from me a much more indignant response when it is offered by people who openly admit that it is not particularly good music. I forbear here even to name any of the organizations which in the third quarter of the twentieth century gave publicity to music of this sort*; but when people produce hymnody in a mood that says, 'This is not good stuff but it will appeal,' they are saying, "It's all they are fit for," which is profanity. I judge it especially wicked so to behave to the young.

If one contrasts the over-enthusiastic and the contemp- 265 tuously trivial with the real masterpieces of twentieth century hymnody, whose popularity is an achievement the seniors among us have actually been able to watch, the formula becomes luminously clear. To take only two: Vaughan Williams's tune (1906) to 'Come down, O love divine' is a tune which brought into currency a text whose author never expected it to be sung, and which now finds its way into most hymnals†. Without any particular kind of

---

* I ought, however, to tell my friends that the attitude I now take to this kind of work is much sterner than that which, I now blush to admit, I took when it was new. One should not be tempted always to say that whatever is new must be given the benefit of the doubt.

---

† Statistics are difficult to come by and do not matter here: the Baptists in America (both conferences) are shy of it. But as a matter of history I venture to record that when it was sung at my own wedding in 1944 it was perfectly familiar to the seminarians present in our college chapel, but quite unknown to any of the rest of the congregation, who were in fact Congregationalists. Since then it has come a long way.

artificial promotion, it has made firm and steady progress. Technically, it meets the worshiper by making a new, good and authentic experience available to him. The meter is unusual — indeed, unique; the composer condenses the long lines and expands the short ones to help the singer. The modest demeanor of the text is reflected in the minute strokes of genius that the tune shows, such as the placing of the one interval in the first phrase that is not taken by step, and the placing of the very important note (and harmony) at the opening of the fifth phrase. This is a perfect example of that combination of restraint and genius which makes a successful and enduring hymn tune.

Alongside it, with only a minimal sense of risk, I should place the tune VINEYARD HAVEN composed in 1974 by Richard Dirksen for 'Rejoice, ye pure in heart,' It is worthy of a less platitudinous text, but the text is one very well known to Americans (although its origin is Victorian English — within two years of that of the text we have just dealt with). It is a text the American congregation would want to sing at the enthronement of a Presiding Bishop in Washington Cathedral, which was the occasion that inspired the tune.* Here again is a tune which 'takes' at once with any congregation. (Despite its recent appearance I have heard it not only on a large academic occasion, and in an enthusiastic campus chapel, but in a parish church accompanied on an inaudible temporary organ). Here again, by the exercise of a truly pastoral imagination which will tell what people will enjoy singing, and of the kind of structural technique which is nearer the art of the watchmaker than that of the bridge-builder, the composer has written what musicians respect and what non-musicians enjoy. <sup>266</sup>

It is not surprising, of course, that successful music for hymns is so often written by organists, or by musical clergymen, who spend so much of their lives in a worshiping congregation. They, after all, know better than the non-worshiping musicians what an ordinary churchgoer 'brings with him'. But they, by virtue of their calling and of the very situation which gives them this advantage, are not infrequently in danger of aiming too low. An organist who never hears anything from his congregation except how much they liked it when he played Easthope Martin's *Evensong* or when the choir sang 'All in an April evening' may allow his hopes for the best in a singing congregation to be dimmed; a parson who has spent much of his time pleasing an unbiddable congregation, <sup>267</sup>

---

* *Westminster Praise* #1: it is the tune I was mentioning in §142.

121

making things easy for them, avoiding disputes and conflicts, will similarly take a fairly cautious view of what they will rise to in music. J.B. Dykes, Precentor of Durham and Vicar of St. Oswald's in that city, who wrote more popular hymn tunes than any composer outside the Gospel Song group (and arguably as many both popular and good as Vaughan Williams), was subject to this defect, and most of his contemporaries in the organ loft or the pulpit were much worse examples of it than he. The unruffled atmosphere of the Victorian parish church tended to confuse contemplation with the avoidance even of legitimate discord, and certainly of undue spiritual effort; and that was not good for any of the arts brought into the church's service at the time. I am reminded here of the very wise remark of Daniel Jenkins (a remark which, like its source, has been attended to far less than it deserves),* that if a preacher's words are always, constantly and immediately understood by all his congregation he may be falling short of his duty as a preacher. It is one of the qualities most to be praised about the 'Come down, O love divine' tune that it disdained any devices of immediate attractiveness.

For this reason, it is both unwise to be absolutely sure that the   268 tune you have just heard and admired is a winner, and to be absolutely sure that something that even to an expert appears obscure and forbidding will not prove to be exactly what another generation wants. The antidote to a too-consenting view of what the people are 'bringing with them', to which traditional worshipers are tempted, could well be the less prejudiced approach of somebody outside the 'family'. What is certain is that, in religious aesthetic, a too restricted and possessive 'family' attitude to the congregation is suffocating (see § 227 above).

But to turn now to other forms of music-making in church,   269 we shall find that the secret of 'reaching out for the best' is the clue here too. The problems of choice range in complexity from the comparatively free range of the cathedral evensong, where the director of music has a trained choir to perform what he selects, and where it is understood that the congregation's participation is purely contemplative, to what I believe to be the very difficult problem of professional church music in protestant churches, especially American.

A Cathedral Office set to music really presupposes that the   270 choir are the worshipers, and that anyone else overhears them. To call it a 'sacred concert', as some frivolously do, is to miss that

---

* *The Protestant Ministry,* Faber Ltd., 1954

point totally. The problem for certain kinds of modern Christians is to accept the notion that anyone who is not part of the choir can worship at all. But of course, such people can, if they know what is required of them (and if they let the Precentor of Coventry, quoted in § 211, help them). The cathedral choir is really like (though it doesn't sound like) the parish congregation singing its hymns; but being trained musicians under constant direction, and being concerned in the continuing of a routine of worship rather than in the seeking of personal inspiration, they are also like the composer himself. If duty is made by music into delight, that is their privilege. In terms of 'inspiration', it is all very low-key activity: in terms of professional discipline, it could hardly be higher. But if it be asked who is communicating what to whom, the answer, in terms Cathedral musicians would accept, is that the carrying on of this ageless and timeless conversation is communicating something to the world around: to have people doing that is as much an effective nourisher of society as it always was when cathedral offices were recognized in the middle ages as the prayers of the whole surrounding community being offered to God by people who were set aside to offer them. What is communicated to society at large (whether it wants to hear it or not) is that it will go sour without prayer: if prayer is made more real, more communicable, by music, so much the better. Enough people who are not choristers are personally in sympathy with this view, however they would themselves express it, to assure, so far, the surprising success of modern appeals for the restoration of cathedral fabrics, if not the problematic future of choir schools.

It is when we come out of the cloister into the parish, and 271 from there to the large American protestant church, that we suddenly run into more formidable difficulties. In the opening pages of this essay I referred to the 'music sprawl' of which I have been made vividly conscious in the United States where churches remain prosperous and populous enough to support a large music program. The kind of experience I referred to in § 5-7 is one which leaves me, as a faculty member in an institution devoted to the pursuit of sacred music, in a thoroughly ambiguous position. Before we can find our way through this particular minefield, some rather unpopular things may have to be said. But instead of laboriously pursuing the fate of choral music through the English parish, via the few nonconformist English and Scottish churches that can run to an efficient choral program to the First Presbyterian Church in this or that American city, I had better go straight to the place where the temperature will be highest.

I have already expressed my admiration and near-envy for 272
American talent in church music. But I am bewildered by the
absence of any connected thought about what, in a protestant
situation, that talent is being used for. American churches seem to
be able, at least in the upper reaches of religious culture, to take
for granted a standard of organ technique and professionalism in
choirmastership which many English cathedrals would respect
and which only a handful of British parish churches can dream of.
I add that certain gifts which I expect, and find in the middle
reaches of English church-musicianship, I tend to encounter
among the black Christians and the Southern Baptists. I particularly refer to the ability to accompany hymns in a manner that
encourage a congregation to sing. But that apart — what is all this
talent *doing*?

Observation tells me that it is doing a good deal that is not 273
specifically musical. An American protestant church may be a
large organization, of 1,500 to 3,000 members perhaps; but its
behavior is often very much based on that of much smaller protestant groups to which the English are accustomed. Conse-
quently the musicians, and their director, hold a place of honor:
they are *prima facie* enjoyed and respected in the community. If
honor of any sort comes to them from outside, the community
shares in it. Their performances therefore, Sunday by Sunday,
reinforce the general sense of community. They are missed if they
are off duty. In many churches there are several choirs, often
graded by age-groups. A choir of teenagers ('high school' in
America) commands the special respect due to any youngster who
has not gone off the rails socially; a choir of younger children is
rejoiced in because they are children; a choir of very young children produces the sort of pleasure people take in young children
— and so on. None of this is in itself particularly reprehensible,
even if, taken too far, it may reinforce the tendencies of some large
churches towards becoming self-sufficient, inward looking and, in
a lofty way, unneighborly.* But with the best will in the world we
cannot claim that any of this brings us very near central issues of
worship.

It is in England rather than in America that one encounters 274

---

* I do not find that Americans have much experience of those special
  pleasures available to their less affluent English cousins who, often
  unable to do much musically in a local church, get a great deal of fun
  and profit out of performances by grouped choirs, from the occasional
  joining of two neighboring churches to the excellent diocesan festivals
  regularly promoted by the Royal School of Church Music.

124

the occasional outspoken comment of a worshiper in this sort of church that the choir bores him; that is a consequence of the very highly developed faculty in the English for being bored. But are any chances being missed? Well; manifestly they are, but to recover them might easily involve some churches in a radical program of intellectual and devotional reconstruction.

Exactly what happens when the choir (whichever of the 275 choirs it is) sings an anthem? What does the *Worshipbook* of the Presbyterian Church give us in the way of guidance? It provides for an Anthem at two points in the order of worship for the Lord's Day: after the Old Testament Lesson, 'a hymn, anthem or psalm', and during the collection of money which precedes the Offertory, 'an anthem or other appropriate music'. That is, an anthem is equivalent to a congregational song as a 'Gradual', between the scripture readings; it is equivalent to a professional piece (the only alternative, presumably, being organ music) while people are presenting their gifts. In practice, in Presbyterian and other churches of similar approach, the anthem at the Offertory seems to be entirely normal, and the other anthem may shift from one point to another in the service. This is understandable: it is easier to go through the technique of putting money in a basket while other people are singing than while you are singing yourself.* But while provision for an offertory hymn is not made in the *Worshipbook,* probably because the use of Ken's doxology remains so universal as a congregation's song at that point, the anthem elsewhere is regarded as an alternative to congregational song. This is important.

The United Reformed Church in England and Wales, whose 276 approach to these things is somewhat different from that found in America despite the Presbyterian tradition that is common to it and to the editors of the *Worshipbook,* offers a fresh clue in § 12 of the Notes preceding its Order of Worship for the Lord's Day† where its spokesman wrote: 'If an anthem is sung it should be included at whatever point in the service it is most appropriate. If

---

* Anglicans in England never think so; but their customs are based on the activity of putting coins in bags, which is much easier to do when you are standing and singing a hymn than putting bills in baskets. Perhaps economics will dictate a different approach when inflation brings the basket to the English parish.

---

† Published 1974 by the United Reformed Church, 86 Tavistock Place, London W1H 9RT. The 'Notes' form a particularly useful guide to the form and principles of worship for a congregation to study.

125

it is a Scripture passage set to music it may even on occasion serve as a substitute for one of the readings.'

That tells us something else about what an anthem is. It is, or may be, a reading of Scripture to music. Obviously it is not that always, because many anthems take hymn texts, or, in older examples, prayers, or, in twentieth century examples, poems for their texts. The United Reformed Church would be unlikely to suggest the substitution of Mundy's 'O Lorde the Maker of all thing' for one of the required prayers; but if they had thought of it they might well have said that the anthem can be compared to the reading of extra-Biblical material in the course of worship — a matter which has properly attracted the attention of liturgists elsewhere. 277

The point of these two examples is to see in what sense liturgical architects in our time think the anthem can be of use. All they have said, but they have converged on the point, is that it can on occasion be a reading, and indeed an interpretation, of Scripture. It must be said that if Scripture is sung at all (otherwise than when psalms are sung to plainsong) there will be an element of interpretation which there would not be in the straight reading of the passage; and indeed I have sometimes said that when an anthem ingeniously places together many passages of scripture (there are not many but two famous examples are John Ireland's 'Greater love hath no man...' and S.S. Wesley's 'Thou wilt keep him in perfect peace') they almost make it possible to dispense with the sermon. 278

But if an anthem is a composition which brings music to the fore, how does it minister to the unmusical? The answer must be (all social considerations apart) through its text. It is therefore an elementary principle that whenever an anthem is sung, the text should be in the hands of all listeners, whether or not the choir regard this as an implied criticism of their diction. It is further required that the anthem's music should be a faithful and modest interpretation of the text — less dependent than a concert-piece may be on massive or surprising effects; but any distinction it may have in that area will be appreciated by the musical only. The rest must be assisted, as best we can, in getting the message that comes from the text. 279

There is rarely any problem about the text's quality because it will normally be scriptural or liturgical. Abominations like 'All in an April evening' and pompous bluster like the text of Charles Wood's musically splendid anthem, 'O thou the central orb' can fortunately be regarded as rare and easily avoidable. (All we need 280 is a good new text for Charles Wood's piece: the other we can forget). But its appropriateness must always be scrutinized, and congregations should be educated to expect textual appropriateness. The distance between the horrific example I quoted in § 7 and the sensitive approach of so many modern American choir directors to the liturgical suitability of anthems is something to be praised and to rejoice in. But as musicians those directors need also to be sensitive to the aesthetic proportions of what they choose. Anthems, to be useful liturgically, must not be too long, or too demonstrative. For example, that magnificently ceremonial piece, Parry's 'I was glad' (one of the very few pieces by that composer known in America) makes a grand opening for a service on the massive scale of an English Coronation or the opening of Coventry Cathedral; in the course of an ordinary Lord's Day service it is likely to be overpowering. It is, of course, the gentle and disciplined understatement of the Tudor musicians, and of some of the Restoration musicians in England and their continental contemporaries, which make their work so universally suitable for liturgical use, and it is good to see so much more attention given to them in these days. This is so much better than the flatulent style of a later period which so often produced pieces with twenty words of text which took several minutes to sing. And should anybody complain that I here imply a criticism of Handel's Hallelujah Chorus, my reply is that the singing of that piece is a folk-gesture, not a devotional exercise, and that I should be appalled at its use as a liturgical anthem, even if it makes a tolerable letter-off of communal steam when sung at the end of an Easter service or as part of a celebration devoted explicitly to music.

Two points emerge from this. The first is to urge choir 281 directors always to consider the unmusical when choosing their anthems; not, of course, to pander to a depressed taste, but rather to have in mind somebody whose attitude to music is purely neutral. The ordinary worshiper will be reached best by anthems which manifestly form part of the 'script' of the service, which perhaps even for the musically unlettered convey some added sense which assists the words to make their message understood, and which do not unduly disturb for him the natural rhythms of devotion. (So many fine pieces come into this category: it is impossible to think of the sound of Peter Hurford's 'In the hour of my distress' failing to arouse some response in the most philistine of listeners).

The second is to ask such directors always to have in mind the 282 ancient function of the anthem, which is to add a decorative emphasis to some important thing that the liturgy is saying. When the 1662 Prayer Book in England first introduced the historic rubric, 'in choirs and places where they sing, here followeth the anthem', it was accepting a practice current even in that church since 1549 of singing sentences in praise of the Virgin Mary at Compline: a concession to any who found some defect in the exclusive use of Old Testament words for praise in those services. But earlier than that, 'anthem' meant 'antiphon' and referred to responsory psalms which were appropriate to the seasons of the church year. These more directly illustrate our main point; they reminded the singers and other worshipers of the thing that that particular act of worship was saying.

The most accessible source for a study of these ancient 'anthem' texts is in that neglected part of the *English Hymnal* which begins at #657. Close attention to this is perhaps the best easy prescription for anyone who would reconstruct his thinking about what anthems are for.

But it may also have this effect on him. He may begin to ask whether the time and location given to anthems in traditional protestant services cannot as profitably be used for psalmody; or for the kind of music which is beginning to be taken notice of now in which both choir and congregation have their parts. I would refer to the responsive psalmody of Joseph Gelineau, current now for a quarter of a century, which gives such ample opportunities for the true meeting of congregation and choir (even for that dangerous creature, the choir soloist); or there are pieces like Malcolm Williamson's *Psalm 121*, which gives the congregation a simple phrase to interpolate in the choral setting;* or again, the hymn 'Rejoice with us in God the Trinity'†, combining the finest work of Frederick Pratt Green the English hymn writer and of John Wilson, the English composer and hymnodist, splendidly sets a simple and sturdy congregational tune over against a choral flourish which only a choir can sing. There is plenty of music of this kind, and although the antiphonal principle goes back to the Catholic middle ages, it is Protestants who may well find it especially an answer to their needs.

---

* It is slightly embarrassing to have to admit that the congregational repetition of this phrase to the words, 'I will lift up mine eyes unto the hills' is liable to perpetuate a misunderstanding of the meaning of the psalm.

---

† *Westminster Praise*, #11

If all that was an attempt to re-establish the choir as a    285
thoroughly edifying adornment of worship, and to urge choristers
and their directors to re-think their role in terms of the needs of the
congregation, what would one say to instrumentalists? The chief
instrumental music maker in church is the organist, and while
there is everything to be said for the occasional use of other
instruments in church, practicalities usually dictate that their use
shall be only occasional. Even if any church could run a resident
orchestra that made a tolerable sound, or even a handful of
resident soloists, it is the organ, with its sustained tone and its
command of tonal variety, that best supports the musical needs of
the liturgy. It may be a bad organ, it may be badly played — in
either case it will fall short of its proper role; but a decent instrument properly played has a case in its favor which will stand up
against all the guitar-enthusiasts who march against it.*

When the organist is playing the accompaniment of an    286
anthem, all we ask of him is that he play it — and edit it sensitively
if he plays from a two-stave score. But his real meeting with the
worshiper will be when he is playing by himself, or when he is
accompanying hymns. In both these areas we should be entering
on an area distractingly technical if we went into them in any
depth; but there are one or two matters which I understand to be
controversial in which our formula may help.

Not much can be said for eighteenth century liturgical habits    287
in England, but at least the churches of that time which had organs
do seem to have given a reasonable sense to the 'organ voluntary'.
This was an organ solo played afte the reading of the Gospel at
Morning or Evening prayer. There being, in those offices, no
sermon, this provided the people with a space for meditation.
Examination of the compositions actually written for this purpose
by people like Purcell and Croft and Boyce shows that they were
modest and undemonstrative pieces, full of eighteenth century
reticence and formality, and not particularly suitable for an organ
recital designed to excite deep musical apprehensions. But as
'background music' they were, of course, just right. There seems to

---

* If an organ simply cannot be obtained, the best alternative is a cappella
singing; failing that, a good piano — but it cannot be too strongly
emphasized (a) that a good piano is expensive, and (b) that the pianist
must be a very skillful arranger. The straight, flat playing of hymn tunes
on a piano is one of the mose depressing sounds in the world, especially
in a building of any size which emphasizes the dying tone of the
piano-string and makes it sound pale and remote if no pianistic technique is brought to bear.

be a case for re-examining our custom of playing while the congregation enters, and while they leave, but never while they are present.* In some places one may even hear a Church Sonata of Mozart, played on appropriate instruments, used for the same purpose, and again it is just the kind of undemonstrative music that suits the purpose. That master of multi-level music, J.S. Bach, of course, provides in his chorale-preludes the ideal music for hearing after the Gospel, not least because it is based on Christian hymns, and even when not everybody present appreciates the inwardness of Bach's thought, nobody present will fail to get something from him. Suppose, for example, the narrative of the healing of the blind men in St. Matthew 20 is the appointed Gospel: and a note in the Bulletin reminded the worshiper that in the original text of this we have the oldest sacred source for the words 'Kyrie eleison', and that the organist was going to play one of the Kyries from the *Klavierübung Part III* — what illumination might such a performance provide? Or if Parry's immortal prelude, 'When I survey the wondrous cross'† were associated with a reading from the Passion story?

Failing this, some use can be made of the incoming and out- 288 going music. Harvey Grace, the most articulate cathedral organist of his age (the 1920s) used to counsel his disciples to play quietly before and after the service; to remember that people were trying to say their prayers; not even to distract them by playing pieces founded on their favorite hymn tunes; and to wait, if they meant to play a rousing piece at the end, until those who wanted to complete their devotions had done so. There was much sense in this, although I know that many distinguished organists in America would disagree with it. But one does have to ask — if you, the organist, are really considering the effect of what you are doing on those who do not particularly appreciate music, what are you likely to do? Of course, one can make an exception of some particularly festive service, or of a service of such massive proportions that some people must wait twenty minutes before it begins: in such cases a decently-appointed short recital is certainly not out of place. But even such a recital can suitably end quietly and in the

---

* In England often, in America rarely, as we have seen, organ music 'covers' the Collection. That is just about all it does: nobody ever thinks of relaxing into music as a contribution to worship.

---

† the F minor one, op. 198, not the better known one on ROCK-INGHAM, which does not have this association in America.

ordinary way; if there is music at all while people enter, it is probably more comfortable for people to be welcomed with a restrained music-pattern (again, Bach and his predecessors serve us so well here) than with a fanfare. A point to bear in mind, too, is that organ music that calls for a loud tone sounds very different when the organ is speaking in a stone cathedral from the way it does when the instrument is in an acoustically dead church, very close to the congregation, and constructed in the assertive tonal style that modern organ builders affect.

When we come to the playing of hymns, there seems to be special difficulty in many parts of America in applying our formula. This is a subtler art than I believe most authorities accept. I venture to criticize most performances I hear in this field for being too noisy and too insensitive; but since I understand that exactly the principles I object to are those largely defended in our organ departments, it is unwise of me even to say the little that I venture to say here: it would be safer either to devote a whole book to the subject (and be execrated for my pains) or to be silent. None the less, I think it is within my brief to say something. 289

What I ask for is simply that organists be encouraged to think pastorally about accompanying congregations; to ask how one sets about encouraging not very musical people to enjoy singing. Some will enjoy it despite the worst pedantries or infelicities of their organist. Far more, I think, would sing if one or two things were borne in mind. 290

In the first place, an organist has to know when to lead and when to encourage. Plenty of things dissuade people from singing. One is a tune they do not know very well. (What are you taught to do to help them in that situation?) Another is being drowned by oppressive sound with which they cannot hope to compete, and which is probably damaging their ears. (What are you taught about the relative value of legato and staccato, and the application to hymns of those rhythmical devices you use in playing Messiaen or Bach?) A third is a dull uniformity of tone, which often comes from the habit of playing throughout on basically the same tonal foundation, varying it only by the occasional addition of a noisier stop. (Is the use of those valuable devices, combination pistons, which set up contrasting tones at the touch of a button, ever mentioned in connection with the playing of hymns?). But the greatest discouragement of all is impalpable: it is the communicating to the congregation of the attitude that says, 'This is uninteresting stuff played for uninteresting people; all I can do is get them through it as quickly as I can.' 291

Anyone who has put in as many hours as I have in church 292
knows quite clearly when the organist is uninterested in people.
But once again we have to apply a brake, because I well know that
what we must call a foreign style of hymn playing is regarded in
America with deep suspicion, and I know on what a solid base this
suspicion rests. If Americans are excellent in technique, and some
from other places are better in imagination, the foreign organists
are liable to be as defective in technique as are those I am criticiz-
ing in interpretation. It is certainly no use being so interested in
expressiveness that you never trouble to play the right notes; being
so skillful in free harmonization that you forget to give warning to
part-singers to sing in unison; being so preoccupied with effect
that elementary techniques are disregarded. Indeed the great fault
of organists who would agree with my protest against pedantic
dullness is that in an overbearing way they can indulge themselves
by 'programming' their victims in exactly the way that we have
said to be forbidden to true artists, back in § 89.

Vulgar self-display, only too possible on the organ, is an 293
obvious and elementary kind of 'programming', of forcing personality where it is out of place, and it is an equally elementary
warning where it is discouraged. But the truth is that those who
really do so play as to encourage unmusical people to sing, and to
bring out the best in them (which of course is not the approach to
communal singing associated with political rallies, football
matches or, I am afraid, revivalist meetings) are people who study
the 'second process' in our formula (§§ 78-9) no less closely when
doing so than when playing as recital virtuosi. Actually, a relaxing
of the standards of discipline and reason which govern that second
process will induce in any singing body exactly the same attitudes:
it will not liberate them but encourage them in their turn to be
programmers in their own way. This is why in the tradition of
Christian worship high-voltage evangelical piety has so often
accompanied a closed mind, an autocratic manner, and a neglect
of the courtesies of Christian discourse in those who embrace it.

All of which is to say that fundamentally our original 294
formula, with its disciplines that serve the liberation of others, and
its service of the kind of liberation that is not self-seeking but
infectious and communicable through all the complexities of
human life, applies to the practical duties of worship just as much
as it applies anywhere else.

# XII
## Experiment and Mystery

Two great matters now await discussion. We have said little 295
yet about 'experimental worship' of the kind in which so much
interest has been shown, and we have hardly so much as mentioned the central act of the Church's worship, which is the Eucharist. It seems appropriate to juxtapose these two notions, which
might appear to be as far from each other as they well could be, in
order to bring what we are saying about communication towards
its completion.

In a sense any form of worship which is unfamiliar is experi- 296
mental; and the word has been used both of forms of worship
which are radical innovations and of forms designed for more
permanent use but offered to Christian communions as 'trial
rites.' From the worshiper's point of view there is little to choose
between them.

Two rather different forces have been at work during the later 297
twentieth century in liturgical thinking and practice. One is the
examination of old and tried forms, containing the question
whether they communicate to our age what they communicated to
the ages for which they were devised; the other is a movement
towards the adjustment of language, based on the conviction that
beyond a certain point, the language of the past is liable to induce
misunderstanding in people of the present.

If this is to be regarded as an ongoing process which is never 298
inoperative, one must admit that its progress has been jerky.
Liturgical experiments or expressions of restlessness were far
from being unknown in the eighteenth century Church of
England.* These were neither very radical nor successful. Certainly the far more searching alterations in Anglican custom
proposed by the Tractarians in the nineteenth century would have

---

* W. Jardine Grisbrooke, *Anglican Liturgies of the Seventeenth and
Eighteenth Centuries* (S.P.C.K., 1958)

impressed worshipers as experimental — and many of them as perniciously experimental. In nonconformity it is difficult to speak of experiments or reforms in what basically does not exist, but such ideas as those put about by Thomas Binney, at the same time that the Tractarians were making their opinions known to anglicans, including the possibility of singing psalms to anglican chants and that of using prayers which were not extempore, will have seemed equally surprising to his constituents; since, however, in nonconformity (Methodism apart) there was no question of any requirement that a custom initiated in one place should become universal, these were not matters that affected many people, and such 'experiments' were things you could always escape from.

Compared with this, the experience of our own century has been revolutionary. From the shy and hesitant efforts of dissenting denominations in the early years to produce directories of worship which were wholly permissive to the much weightier pronouncements of their assemblies nearer our own time has been a considerable stride. Moreover, the existence of the International Consultation on English in the Liturgy has persuaded many Christian groups to take into their own systems liturgical formulae approved for use by vernacular-speaking Catholics. The Common Lectionary is gaining ground; with a few notable exceptions, the common Canon of the Eucharist has come a long way. (At the time of this writing the text of the Lord's Prayer seems to be as unlikely to reach general acceptance as it ever was.). For much of this we can thank the dissipation by the Ecumenical Movement of superstitious errors in the thinking of nonconformist protestants about Anglican and Catholic forms of worship; and Vatican II, of course, gave it an enormous impetus. The results of it, however, strike worshipers still as 'experimental.'

In Anglican circles, so much that has more recently been done for non-anglicans was achieved by the Tractarians that the only liturgical innovation before the Second World War, the 1928 Prayer Book, proved to be hardly more radical than the 1881 Revised Version of the Bible. (It made a stir at the time because Parliament vetoed it; but the resultant discussion was much less about liturgy than about the issue of Establishment.). So the Church of England's chief experience of experiment has been in our second category — the rewriting of the liturgies in modern speech. Catholics were granted the right to use the vernacular in worship just at the time when in other circles this linguistic upheaval was at its fiercest.

The linguistic revolution probably has its efficient cause 301
in the new attitude to sacred texts generated by the Higher Criticism of the Bible, which in its turn produced first the Revised Version, then a short series of new translations of which Moffatt's was the most celebrated, and now, more lately, a very large number of new versions. We have said enough about it (§ 245-9) to make any further discussion of the use of modern English unnecessary; it is here brought back into the picture because of its relation to the whole concern of 'experiment'.

We have indeed, already said that pitfalls appear in the path 302
of any who claim that the translation of the mysteries of our faith into modern speech will at once remove all chance of their being misused or misinterpreted. Now we must press home our contention that if experiments are to liberate, their promoters, local or ecumenical, need to make some very close and anxious decisions. Above all, they need to be quite clear in what they believe about the place of *understanding* in worship.

Paul, in the passage we quoted and have since referred to 303
constantly (I Cor. 14) places understanding in a position subordinate to *edification* (which we interpret as the nourishment of maturity). Let us suppose that worship, being designed to nourish believers in their quest for maturity, is required among other things to nourish their minds. If that is so (I hold it) then we are hoping that our worship systems will assist our people in becoming wise. But is it not a fact known to humanists as well as Christians that the wise person is the person who knows how much he does not know, and is constantly open to new knowledge and new surprises exacting from him the tribute of repentance and even of altering views to which his wisdom up to that moment seemed to bring him? In other disciplines that is so evident as to be a platitude. The question for any 'experimenter' who defies a tradition must be whether his offerings will mislead less, and nourish more, than that which he is altering. If it is truly to nourish wisdom, will it be enough if it is merely intelligible? May it not (as in § 267 above) be dangerous if it is totally and immediately and effortlessly intelligible?

But what is 'intelligible'? In any great matter, it is that which 304
arouses a response of intelligence: which is to say, it arouses a 'YES!' At the highest level, we are saying that it arouses a 'YES!' followed at once by a sense of responsibility to spread the experience gained in it by extinguishing the 'I'. We have said that constantly. It now turns out to what many humanists know more about than Christians know. For we have also said that a certain

kind of over-cautiousness about being sure one is understood and accepted is fatal to true communications. And we can now say that if the communicator treats the recipient of his message as somebody who is merely seeking information to store, instead of seeking truth to share, he will extinguish the Holy Spirit's work before it has had a chance to begin.

Liturgical change, therefore, becomes necessary from time to 305 time in order that the legitimate right of people to 'understand' is not jeopardized. But the experience of these recent years in which liturgical change has been, in some form, the experience of so large a proportion of English-speaking Christians has shown that the shoe pinches unexpectedly. For liturgy depends for its effectiveness to a greater degree on custom than many who advocated change in it had realized. The familiar liturgy of 1662-1928 is as precious to many anglicans as the familiar hymns are to many protestants. This is not in any way to say that either anglicans or protestants who feel that way are being culpably conservative. The assimilation of what is unfamiliar requires a mental activity which, while it is certainly not an irretrievable distraction from worship, does use up energy which would otherwise be set free for contemplation. Familiarity of words and forms sets the mind free to 'understand' in a way which impatient reformers always overlook. A delicate balance has to be kept: between the familiarity which engenders mental sloth and the unfamiliarity which excludes all but the very alert.

An analogy may help. It is noticeable how much easier 306 anglicans find it to join an unfamiliar parish when their work or some other need moves them from one place to another than protestants, especially those of the puritan heritage, find it. On the one side you have a tradition which more or less ensures — provided one allows for the large distinction between evangelical and tractarian anglicanism — that in a strange place one will find a familiar liturgy. In consequence, people settle down with satisfaction in the new church which may be the only familiar thing they find in the new place. Conversely the traditional forms of old-style Congregationalism, for example (which provides a more extreme form of the opposite than do the Methodists or the Baptists) almost ensures that the church in the new place will be as unfamiliar as anything else about it; that the newcomer is required to adjust to styles of preaching, service-planning, and church life which may well be very different from what the previous place provided for him. The result is a much greater tendency among Dissenters to drop away, less through laziness than through bewilderment; or, to put it otherwise, the greater vulnerability of these forms of Christian style to the mobility of modern times.

That tells us two things: one is, as we said above, that custom 307 always helps people to receive the communication of liturgy, and the disturbance of custom can radically upset the commitment of Christians to the church. The other is that it is precisely the mobility of modern society that has prompted liturgical reforms in the formerly non-liturgical communions, and that provides one of the most powerful arguments in their favor.

But this means that in order to achieve a measure of cath- 308 olicity that modern society demands, it is necessary for many church groups to alter their way of life in liturgy. When one adds to this the demand of the new-Renaissance twentieth century churchgoer for 'understanding' — a demand we admit often to be misconceived or at least ill-expressed — we have the reason why not only the Dissenting but also the Catholic churches have undergone the reforms with which we are all now familiar.

Transfer, change, and the removal of domestic landmarks, 309 then, bring discomfort, and that must be acknowledged. When a group makes changes in its liturgical customs it is dislodging much that its members held in affection and through which they genuinely worshiped and the effect is as if those people had been moved to an unfamiliar place as well as being faced with unfamiliar demands. Therefore two things are needed in any program of reconstruction if that discomfort is to be reasonably short-lived. The new words and actions must be such as will as soon as possible 'come naturally,' and they must be assisted in their purpose by being, according to our previous formula, works of art. Those who devise them need to have the gift of 'reaching out for the best' in those to whom they minister, and both reason and skill will be required in its application.

It is on grounds such as these that one is entitled to criticize, 310 favorably or adversely, such new liturgies as are now being devised. Much that has been done in the reconstruction of public worship in the major denominations has been rational and admirable. Chief among these points of reconstruction is the head-on attack on the Word-centred, unsacramental habits of the protestants, by promoting as the normal order for the Lord's Day an order for the celebration of Communion, and indicating that where the Sacrament is not celebrated, the liturgy that remains should be an ante-Communion. The most noticeable effect of this is the transferring of the sermon back to a position directly associated with the readings, and the ending of the custom of making it an eminent peak around which all the rest of the service looks like inconsiderable foothills. This was done not least in obedience to history: it made it possible for protestants not only to celebrate properly their Genevan heritage (if they wanted to) but, more importantly, to recover a medieval tradition that is common to all Christendom. (But protestants added responsible preaching: their contribution was by no means submerged in sentimental historicism).

The second very noticeable effect of liturgical change was, as 311 we have said, in the use of language. Here the decisions were subtle, not broad, and taken, in some places, with a less sure touch. Two examples occur to me of decisions that seem to have missed their mark. One of these is in the salutation which occurs at certain points in the Eucharist and the Offices

> The Lord be with you
> And with thy spirit.

Thus translated in the older versions it represents the Latin 'Dominus vobiscum: et cum spiritu tuo.' In the ICEL liturgies this appears as

> The Lord be with you
> and also with you.

The object clearly was to get rid of the expression 'thy spirit', which admittedly is nowadays (and in English always was) a slightly odd reply to the salutation — itself a gracious phrase. The substituted translation translates 'et' by 'and also' — and it is an odd and interesting example of a phrase which probably reads inoffensively but comes very awkwardly when spoken. 'Also' is a word more for writing than for speech, and even in writing needs to be supporting a weightier subordinate clause than it has to support here. For good conversation, 'And with you' would have done very well except that for communal speech it is perhaps too short for comfort. Coventry Cathedral ingeniously gets round the difficulty by substituting a biblical phrase for the old liturgical one:

> The Lord be with you
> The Lord bless you      (Ruth 2.4)

Since this is in context a salutation on meeting, not on parting, it seems ideal for the purpose. The liturgists must have rejected it because they did not wish to disturb the old liturgy by taking out the old formula and substituting another. From the point of view of good natural communal speech it was a pity, and could be judged a needless pedantry.

The other example is the result of the decision of the editors 312
of the *Worshipbook* to use, as far as possible, the J. B. Phillips
translation for New Testament passages incorporated in the
liturgy. This was perhaps the very last translation they should
have chosen, since it was composed not for liturgy but explicitly
for private reading or study. (*Letters to Young Churches* was
originally done for a church youth group in an English parish
where Phillips was rector). The genial talkativeness of that version
— together with its undoubted scholarly insights — makes it
wholly admirable as an ancillary text; but the *Worshipbook* editors found themselves with this, as an announcement of the Assurance of Pardon:

Hear the good news!
This statement is completely reliable and should be
universally accepted: Christ Jesus entered the world to
rescue sinners.

That is a possible translation of the original in I Timothy, but
Phillips surely overreached himself in his choice of words; and
even if they read reasonably well, when spoken they sound like
part of an advertisement for a credit card. Liturgy would have
surely been content with 'Here are words you may trust' (I Tim. 1.
15, NEB), omitting the emphatic phrase following. Liturgy must
never waste words, and it was one of the faults of the *Worshipbook* liturgy (and of so many before it) that it confused clarity
with explanatoriness.

These two very small examples illustrate the point, which has 313
to do with the aesthetic and drama of worship (§195ff) that
liturgical speech, especially when it is put in the mouths of worshipers, must be natural and graceful, never garrulous, never
approximate. It is undoubtedly the failure to appreciate this that
has brought much needless difficulty in the acceptance of new
liturgies, and will, if it is persisted in, cause much of the Holy
Spirit's *élan* to evaporate from the devotion of congregations that
accept them.

That which comes naturally, when offered to a community of 314
people, is actually that which has been scrutinized by very precise
and objective minds. Any kind of preoccupation on the part of
liturgy-writers (and this must apply to any who, in free-style
worship, compose *ad hoc* prayers or responses for their people's
use) will distract them from this concentrated and highly skilled
task. Even the earnest desire to be correct, certainly any desire not
to be misunderstood, any sense of hurry or urgency, any pressure
from public opinion, may be enough to cause the concentration to

falter, and to allow a writer to be content with what actually will not be 'what they were waiting to say' but remains what, with the loftiest intentions no doubt, he wanted them to say. And that is programming.

It is from that ground that one would wish that local experiments in liturgy were scrutinized more carefully than they usually are. It is not seldom the case that these — with novel prayers, novel hymns, and novel approaches to everything, are compiled by people who have not really distinguished between what they would like the congregation to do and what the congregation is waiting to be called on to do. Again we say that nobody should underestimate the content of that 'waiting'. There is no evidence anywhere that congregations prefer what is shoddy if given the choice between it and what is disciplined and graceful. But, aside from the distraction which any congregation must feel when every Sunday service is totally different from any that went before, the tendency to disregard what one could objectively discover to be the best that the people are offering is what makes many of the more irresponsible 'experiments' foolish. 315

It is unlikely that just now it will be acceptable, but none the less I believe it will be later found to be true, that any 'experiment' that depends on the special non-ministerial gifts of, say, a local minister, and that will collapse when he disappears, should be excluded from the normal worship of the Lord's Day. Only that which is demonstrably founded in a tradition the people can be expected to accept and confirm should be permitted. And anything which demands more than the barest minimum of explicit instruction from the leader of worship should be viewed at least with suspicion. For if people are constantly being 'programmed' by their worship leaders, either they will withdraw in discontent, or they will (more probably because of their personal loyalty to the local community) accept a form of worship which in the end is not worship at all, because it leaves them no space for being 'liberated'. It may be high grade entertainment, to which they themselves have contributed a good deal; but as a liberator of the mind and a maker of apostles, it will simply not be functioning. 316

But now we must turn to that central act of worship which can only now really be looked at and appreciated. (All hymnals ought to leave their Communion section to the far end, placing it only before the section on the Beatific Vision and the Blessed Trinity). What can we say about the Eucharist as a vehicle of the divine communication? 317

Well, first, why need we say anything at all? Is not this some- 318
thing better left undiscussed? I fear not. There are too many
faithful church people to whom the Eucharist, though they attend
it, means very little, or nothing, for us to be able to pass it over
here. All of them, in my experience, are protestants, but the very
liturgical reconstructions we have been speaking of seem to indicate that in many regions of Christendom some doubts have
arisen on the question whether the communication is here being
fully achieved.

Since this is not a study in liturgies as such, we can leave on 319
one side all discussion of comparative forms of worship. What we
are asking is what the principle of communication is in this central
sacramental act. And the most evident thing of all is that it is a
*mystery*. That word at once needs explaining.

Classical Greek usage gave the word *mysterion* the meanings 320
of (a) a secret known only to the initiated, and later (b) a secret
known only to the knowledgable but communicable to those
prepared to learn it. In this second sense it was used only when
scientific inquiry had overtaken the classical culture, and it could
mean simply what a learned teacher taught his pupils. In the
earlier sense, which is carried over into the New Testament, it
seems to have meant what anyone who was prepared to be
initiated could acquire, but what was totally hidden from the rest.
Paul uses the word in various shades of meaning: 'Behold, I show
you a mystery' (I Cor. 15:51); 'we speak the wisdom of God in a
mystery: the hidden wisdom of God'(I Cor. 2:7) — as it were; 'You
will understand, but not everybody would': or 'though I have the
gift of prophecy and understand all mysteries'(I Cor. 13:2) — as it
were; 'learning and acuteness are not enough': or the 'speaker in
tongues' — 'howbeit in the spirit he speaketh mysteries' (I Cor.
14:2) — as it were; 'He is keeping to himself what he ought to be
communicating.' Mystery, then, in Paul and elsewhere in the New
Testament is a secret: usually it is a secret revealed to the Christian; more rarely it is either a secret which is kept when it ought to
be shared, or a secret which is not worth exploring.

Now when we said just now that the Eucharist is a *mystery* we 321
were using not a New Testament word but a medieval one. The
Eucharist is not referred to in Scripture as a mystery. The content
of the Faith is called a mystery in I Timothy: the allegories of the
Book of Revelation are called mysteries. But not the Supper itself,
until after the apostolic age.

But if 'mystery' in its most exalted sense is a 'hidden message', 322
then it is exactly what we have been describing as the content of

real communication. The Book of Revelation is indeed a handy example: we have there what appears on the surface to be a fantastic dream, or a piece of primitive science-fiction, but which contains a 'hidden message' for the beleaguered Christians to whom it was written from Patmos by an author who knew his document would have to pass a censor and would be destroyed if it was seen to convey the message it really did convey. It is already obvious that when we were discussing the message of poetry, the preacher's art, the art of liturgy, and the communications of all Scripture, this is what we have been saying. The words clothe and protect a hidden message which is not to be extracted by any who do not know that that is what the words are really for.

The Eucharist as observed by Christians is not merely one 323 more illustration of this. It really is its fountain-head. It will in a little while be clear that it is that in a most unexpected way. But before we get to that climax, let us consider what we mean by saying that the rite is 'mysterious.'

We mean two things, unhappily, and the first is that in many 324 of its current forms it is unintelligible. How is it possible that a confused and perverse form of celebration may still 'mean something' to those who attend it? Because they bring with them some need which they rely on it to satisfy, some loyalty which translates its infelicities. Just as, thanks to the work of the Holy Spirit who does not do all his work through liturgies, there are people whom the most trivial and disreputable preaching will not dislodge from their faith, so the most slovenly and irrational 'celebrations' will not dislodge them either. (Perhaps one has to have been a minister in British nonconformity, and to have a long memory, to know just how much strain good people's faith has had to stand up to in this matter.).

Now I am very grateful to certain American friends, and 325 especially to the teaching of the Reverend Horace T. Allen, Jr., for laying bare an essential clue to the unintelligibility of the Eucharist. I have said in earlier pages some critical things, so it is a pleasure here to record that in this matter the Presbyterian *Worshipbook* (1970) seems to have opened a much needed window. The clue is in that the Eucharist can be, and very often is, too exclusively associated with the Last Supper, and the rubrical announcement called for in the *Worshipbook*'s Service for the Lord's Day immediately under the heading, 'Invitation to the Lord's Table' — which departs from what other ecumenical observances to-day prescribe — shows where the primary emphasis is in the minds of its liturgists. (See page 34 in the 1970 edition).

We are obliged to say — and if we can swallow the rather 326
difficult innovation of detaching the Eucharist from the Last
Supper we can say with a great sigh of freedom — that we do not
know and never shall know exactly what the origin of the Eucharist is. For one thing, scholars still continue to dispute the question
whether it was a Passover meal (in which case it seems to have
been celebrated irregularly, a day before custom demanded it) or
something equally customary but less ceremonious. For another:
if it was a Passover meal it was a very curious one because it was a
group of friends, not a family with its father at the head, who were
celebrating. But more than that: the Synoptic Gospels which
report it (John does not report it all) differ considerably about
what their authors remember. Mark says that Jesus took bread,
gave it to them, and said, 'This is my body', and that he took the
cup of wine, that they drank it, and that after that he said, 'This is
my blood of the (new) covenant, which is poured out for many.'
(The word "new" is not in all the sources of Mark). 'Matthew's
recollection is that Jesus took, blessed and broke bread, and said,
'Take, eat, this is my body;' and that he then took the cup and said,
while giving it to them, 'Drink of it, all of you; for this is my blood
of the (new) covenant, which is poured out for many for the
forgiveness of sins.' Both these evangelists agree in adding that he
said, 'I shall not drink of this fruit of the vine until that day when I
drink it with you in my Father's kingdom.' Luke's account places
the drinking of the wine (with the saying about this being the last
time Jesus will drink it before the Kingdom comes) first, with the
words, 'Take this, and divide it among yourselves,' — but makes
no reference to its being his blood; then the bread is blessed and
broken, and as he gives it to them he says, 'This is my body.' John,
as everybody knows, substitutes the symbolic act of foot-washing
and the long conversation in his chapters 13-17 for everything
reported by the Synoptics.

The points upon which the Synoptics agree, then, are the 327
saying, 'This is my body', applied to the bread, and the oracular
announcement that this marks the boundary between the old
order and the coming of 'The Kingdom' as far as Jesus is concerned. It is St. Paul — admittedly writing before any of the
Gospels reached the forms we know — who introduces the phrase,
'Do this in remembrance of me,' with that telling word 'remember'
which has perhaps done most of the damage. Not — we hasten to
say — that there is anything inauthentic about what Paul writes in
I Corinthians 11; but the word 'remember' must always bear its

full force of 'bringing into the present', not the debased meaning of 'put yourselves back into the past.'

On this evidence, we do not quite know what the Last Supper 328 was as an historical event, or exactly what happened there; yet we could not have been more closely and meticulously informed about what it meant to Jesus and his friends than we are in the conversations which the Synoptics associate with it, and in the long and affectionately-recorded colloquy, ending with that immortal prayer, which are set down in John 13-17. We are liable to be thrown off course, then, if we hang the Eucharist exclusively on the Words of Institution as recorded by St. Paul, and in consequence I now believe the Anglicans to be right in incorporating those words in the Great Prayer, and my own people in error in giving them greater prominence as a rubrical announcement.

The fact is, surely, that just as we do not know exactly what 329 happened at the Nativity, or the Resurrection, or the Ascension, or Pentecost, but base our beliefs in the hidden message which comes so clearly through the evangelists' descriptions of these events, so we do not know, from the text, all that happened at the Last Supper. And therefore, just as we can be thrown off course if we attend too closely and obsessively to the letter of Scripture in the matter of those other events (and in so doing miss what other Scriptures importantly say about them), so this can happen with the Eucharist. How many sentimental sermons have been preached on the phrase, 'No room in the inn', as if the innkeeper was in any sense to blame (he was very sensible and resourceful to find the Holy Family some privacy in the stables); how much needless anxiety has been caused to believers who are prevented from seeing what Scripture as a whole says about the Resurrection and the Ascension by an obsessive preoccupation with the physical mechanics of events so defectively described? How many tongues of fire were there at Pentecost and how were they distributed among the heads?

Speculations of that sort are always futile. Scripture in that 330 mood — the mood it shows when it gives authority for all our great liturgical celebrations — is to be relaxed into, not hectored with speculative questions. (We know that and accept it at Christmas: we are less sure at the other great seasons). But there are two things that can be said, both of which might provide some means of bringing comfort to people for whom the Eucharist has gone pale and dim. Theologically it must be said that this celebration has to do with the present and the future as much as with the past. The other point is perhaps marginal to my own purpose, although it arises directly from what has just been said.

This is to say, with regret and with considerable expectation 331 of being declared a surly critic for saying it, that I do not myself see that there is any more virtue in associating Maundy Thursday with the foot-washing incident in St. John 13 than the Eucharist, on that or any other day, with the Last Supper. If one contrasts the foot-washing ceremony with, say, the observance of Tenebrae (proper to Good Friday though sometimes less appropriately associated with Maundy Thursday), one is contrasting a re-enactment with a symbol. The incorporating of a foot-washing ceremony into the church's rites seems to me to be of doubtful value simply because with the best will in the world nothing in modern life corresponds with the act of foot-washing. When our Lord did it, it was something everybody expected to take place: the surprise was that the wrong person was doing it. It should have been done, they all thought, by a servant. Modern society doesn't use servants in that fashion: people don't, except on vacation, wear sandals on bare feet, and if they do, the places where they walk are not dusty as the old streets were (though they may be dirty in other ways). True, the symbolism of a bishop washing the feet of a junior priest or a lay person has much beauty and tenderness; but that is not enough, as liturgists would in other circumstances be the first to insist, to ensure the validity of the symbol as an act of worship.

But if anyone wants to enter into the church's experience of 332 the Eucharist, such a person must fit the 'remembering' aspect of it in with so much else that is strictly Scriptural and in no sense ecclesiastical accretion. The people who help us to do this are the folk-poets of the Church, the hymn writers. Let us hear them as they speak about this event which is so central to the liturgical life of the congregation.

It is a Passover 'sacrifice': the crude propitiation of the 333 pagan and the Gentile, exalted but not regenerated by Israel, transformed in the innocent sacrifice of Christ — not now a helpless animal laid on an altar and bound by mortals, but — 'No man taketh my life from me: I lay it down of myself.' Sacrifice —and more than sacrifice:

O the sweet wonders of that Cross,
    where Christ my Saviour loved, and died!
Her noblest life my spirit draws
    from his dear wounds, and bleeding side.*


'One offering, single and complete'
    with lips and hearts we say;
but what he never can repeat
    he shows forth day by day.

For as the priest of Aaron's line
    within the holiest stood
and sprinkled all the mercy shrine
    with sacrificial blood;

so he, who once atonement wrought,
    our Priest of endless power,
presents himself, for those he bought
    in that dark noontide hour.

His Manhood pleads where now it lives
    on heaven's eternal throne,
and where in mystic rite he gives
    his presence to his own.†


The smoke of thy Atonement here
    darkened the sun and rent the veil,
made the new way to heaven appear,
    and showed the great Invisible:
well pleased in thee our God looked down
and calls his rebels to a crown.

He still respects thy sacrifice,
    its savour sweet doth always please,
the Offering smokes through earth and skies,
    diffusing love and joy and peace,
to these thy lower courts it comes
and fills them with divine perfumes.‡

---

* Isaac Watts, *Hymns,* Book III (For the Holy Communion), #10: two words altered.

---

† William Bright, *Hymns and Other Poems,* 1866. EH 327.

---

‡ Charles Wesley, *Hymns on the Lord's Supper* (1745). MHB (English) 771.

It is a family at a table:

> Jesus invites his saints
> to meet around his board;
> here pardoned rebels sit and hold
> communion with their Lord. . . .
> Our heavenly Father calls
> Christ and his members one;
> we the young children of his love,
> and he the firstborn Son.*

It is nourishment by a food which does more for the soul than manna did for the starving, frantic Israelites:

> Author of life divine,
>     who hast a table spread,
> furnished with mystic wine
>     and everlasting bread,
> preserve the life thyself hast given
> and feed and train us up for heaven.†

Indeed, it is more than what the psalmist (speaking of manna) called 'angels' food':

> The angelic host above
> can never taste this food;
> they feast upon their Maker's love,
> but not a Saviour's blood.‡

It is the transformation of old rites, framed in fear, into a new rite, conceived in love:

> Therefore we, before him bending,
>     this great Sacrament revere;
> types and shadows have their ending
>     for the newer rite is here;
> faith, our outward sense befriending,
>     makes the inward vision clear.#

---

* Isaac Watts, *Hymns,* Book III # 2 sts 1, 4. CP 295.

---

† Charles Wesley, *Hymns on the Lord's Supper* (1745). EH 303.

---

‡ Isaac Watts, *Hymns,* Book III #17, st 4.

---

# St Thomas Aquinas, for Corpus Christi, c. 1263, tr. J.M. Neale. EH 326.

It is the moment when the human soul becomes one with the
Lord; the moment of ecstatic intimacy:

Sun, who all my life dost brighten;
Light, who dost my soul enlighten;
Joy, the sweetest man e'er knoweth;
Fount, whence all my being floweth:
at thy feet I cry, 'My Maker,
let me be a fit partaker
of this blessed food from heaven,
for our good, thy glory, given.*

It is remembrance:

Thy Body, broken for my sake
my bread from heaven shall be;
thy testamental cup I take,
and thus remember thee.†

It is remembrance that brings up the cosmic act of atonement
into the present:

His dying crimson, like a robe,
spreads o'er his body on the Tree;
then am I dead to all the globe,
and all the globe is dead to me.‡

It is proclamation of the victory of Christ:

It was a strange and dreadful strife
when life and death contended,
but victory remained with life,
the reign of death was ended....

So let us feast this Easter day
on the true Bread of heaven.
The word of grace hath purged away
the old and wicked leaven....#

---

* J. Franck, *Praxis Pietatis Melica* (1653), tr. C. Winkworth, EH 306.

† James Montgomery, *The Christian Psalmist* (1825). EH 300.

‡ Isaac Watts, *Hymns,* Book III #8. EH 107.

# From Martin Luther, *Christ lag* (1524), tr. R. Massie. CP 761.

It is a celebration of victory and of hope; especially a 'fore-taste of the feast of heaven', a celebration of our acceptance of the fact that we are 'waiting'; that it is all, here on earth, 'between the times': as St Paul said, 'You do show forth the Lord's death until he come":

> At thy command, our dearest Lord,
>     we celebrate thy dying feast;
> thy blood like wine adorns thy board,
>     and thine own flesh feeds every guest.
>
> Let the vain world pronounce it shame
>     and fling their scandals on his cause;
> we come to boast our Saviour's name
>     and make our triumph in his cross.
>
> With joy we tell the scoffing age,
>     'He that was dead has left his tomb;
> He lives above their utmost rage
>     and we are waiting till he come.*
>
> Though the cloud from sight received him
>     when the forty days were o'er,
> shall our hearts forget his promise,
>     'I am with you evermore.'?†
>
> O risen Christ, to-day alive,
>     amid your Church abiding,
> who now your blood and body give,
>     new life and strength providing;
> we join in heavenly company
> to sing your praise triumphantly:
>     Lord Christ, we see your glory.‡
>
> Sion hears the watchmen shouting,
> her heart leaps up with joy undoubting,
>     she stands and waits with eager eyes;
> see her Friend from heaven descending,
> adorned with truth and grace unending!

---

\* Isaac Watts, *Hymns,* Book III #19. CP 294.

---

† W. Chatterton Dix, *Altar Songs,* 1867. EH 301.

---

‡ E.R. Morgan (Bishop), 1950; text as *Hymns for Celebration,* 1974, #23.

Her light burns clear, her star doth rise.
Now come, thou precious Crown,
Lord Jesus, God's own Son!
Hosanna!
Let us prepare
to follow there
where in thy Supper we may share.*

It is the Church's experience of a unity denied to her, and to humanity, in this mortal life, but prayed for by her Lord and promised by him:

Whoso of this Food partaketh
rendeth not the Lord, nor breaketh:
Christ is whole to all that taste.
Thousands are as one, receivers,
one, as thousands of believers,
takes the Food that cannot waste.

Good and evil men are sharing
one repast, a doom preparing
varied as the heart of man;
doom of life or death awarded,
as their days shall be recorded
which from the beginning ran.

When the Sacrament is broken
doubt not in each severed token,
hallowed by the word once spoken,
resteth all the true content:
nought the precious Gift divideth,
breaking but the sign betideth,
he himself the same abideth,
nothing of his fulness spent.†

Each of these paragraphs we have introduced with the words 334 "it is. . . ' In what sense, 'is'? We do not mean identity; we do not mean that any of these figures, to which many more could have been added, exhausts the message of the Eucharist; still less do we mean that one is right and the rest wrong. We mean that these are things that the Eucharist has said to the Church, and that the

---

\* Philipp Nicolai, *Freudenspiegel,* 1597, tr F.C. Burkitt. EH 12.

---

† St Thomas Aquinas, for Corpus Christi, c. 1263: from *Lauda Sion,* EH 317.

Church has said to the Eucharist. It is these things, and so much more like them, things that only poets can communicate and only the greatest of hymn writers articulate for the Christian congregation, that have brought the Eucharist from being a love-feast in the catacombs to the medieval Mass, the puritan Lord's Supper, the evangelical Meal of Fellowship, the parish Communion.

The only question we are attacking is whether anything can 335 be said to comfort those to whom the Eucharist means little, or those who are concerned that it does not mean as much as it might to their people. And we have invoked not theologians but poets to answer it. The truth which they attest is surely this: that for the proper communication of the truth of the Gospel — anywhere, but supremely at this point — it is not enough to have definition; we must have space. Imagination must be allowed to live freely with dogma; faith with reason.

There is, I think, an analogy to be drawn from another field 336 of devotion. We are aware that the English word 'love' has to do duty for at least four Greek words (is this a curious testimony to the inhibitedness of English thought and conversation on this subject?).* The Greek words are *philia, eros, storge* and *agape*; and very roughly they mean the love one has for friends, for a spouse, for children, and — ah! for what? The fourth category is very simply distinguished from the other three: the first three are, as it were, quantitative; whoever loves has only so much love to go round, and there is a limited supply for its objects. One can love (Christians say) only one spouse, and not an infinite number of friends or a limitless family. But that which St. Paul celebrates in I Corinthians 13 is inexhaustible. It does not diminish, but increases, with the number of objects it has. Directed towards a single person it is indistinguishable from the others. The broader its field, the richer it gets. That is what we mean by the distinction.

In the handling of the things we call 'mysteries,' there is an 337 analogous pattern. In certain fields of discourse, if this is right, that cannot also be right. There is, as it were, a quantitative kind of 'rightness' which cannot include in its field concepts that contradict each other. That is the field of reason. In 'mysteries' it is not so. Now all those figures under which we reprsented the Eucharist are categories of experience; they are what it has said to people. And it is very familiar that some kinds of people lean towards some of those categories and away from others: that you could

---

* I follow C.S. Lewis's four rather than the traditional three of moralists. See *The Four Loves* (1960)

almost draw up a table with those categories on one side and a series of temperaments on the other. You could certainly say that traditions have favored some and rejected others; that the puritans saw it as a family meal and the traditional Catholics as a mystical sacrifice; and that it is difficult to see how any one person can possibly see it as both. But that is where we need to be careful. It is no offence to reason to say that a subject like the Eucharist can be represented under so many different figures, any more than it was an offense to reason to describe God in as many affectionate and reverential terms as the Old Testament writers allowed themselves to use.

If one analyzes a Eucharistic liturgy in other planes, of course, 338 one does find categories that are, as it were, quantitative and in a sense exclusive. The Common Liturgy of our time is more or less settling down, in all the major denominations, into a liturgical pattern of five 'movements': Approach, the Hearing and Preaching of the Word, Offertory, Communion and Withdrawal. Those movements, each described by naming an activity at least partly human, are rational and convenient. It is very proper that you should save intercession for the Offertory section, that you should expound Scripture immediately after reading it, and so on. These are not mysteries but serviceable instructions or customs. But what has gone wrong in church relations — what has caused the Sacrament of Unity to become historically the very point at which Christian groups divided — has been the insistence that if you believe this then you cannot possibly believe that as well. True; some of the controversies were reducible to reason, and there were points at which people in error had to be shown that they were believing two contradictory propositions at the same time; and this is what the leading Reformers made it their business to do. But if one is not blessed with minds as acute as those of Luther and Calvin (and, I have to say, even if one is) it is difficult not to mix the categories, and to apply that exclusiveness which pertains to reason to areas where it is irrelevant.

But if we may bring this down to a single point, we shall find 339 that even there we are making a needless allowance for the zeal of rationalists and reformers. Take the subject of transubstantiation. Now this is a philosophical proposition which states that at the moment of Consecration at the Eucharist the substance of the Elements is changed while their accidents remain unchanged. It is a statement as rational as that, and depends for its intelligibility on an understanding of the difference in logic between substance and accident. The difference broadly is that anything that can be

152

sensibly appreciated, like color, texture, weight, smell, shape, is an accident; what is left when you have stripped all that away from, in this case, bread and wine, is substance: substance is always impalpable, apprehensible only by intellect, and nameable only with such absurd-sounding words as 'breadness' and 'wineness'. When Dr. Nathaniel Micklem, slightly mischievously, said in one of his essays that he (a protestant divine) understood transubstantiation but he doubted whether most Catholics did, he was stating a very probable notion: most people are not trained in academic logic, though he had been.

Now this happens to have been one subject upon which the 340 Reformers were in dispute with the Catholic Church, because they denied that it made any kind of sense. The Catholic position was that the Elements became the Body and Blood of Christ, while not being changed in any way appreciable by human sense. But nobody has ever actually produced a more intelligible formula for interpreting the "is" in 'This is my Body.' Far from attempting to behave like helpless dogmatists, the scholastics who produced that formula knew perfectly well that they were explaining what cannot be explained.

But an artist could have explained it. For if we call to 341 mind what was said a good deal earlier in our investigations (§§ 29ff, ch 5) about the journey made by a message, what we said was that a word, or a sound, or a message, is constructed with care and then sent on its way to a destination unknown to the artist, or, even if the destination is known, that what happens to it when it arrives is, and must always be, outside the artist's control. We said that the hope of the communicator was that it would arouse an 'I' and a 'YES!' in the person who received it. Suppose then that we ask, what change has taken place in that message between the time it was sent and the time the 'YES!' was given? It is the same words, the same sounds; it has been given its motive power by the originator's skill, so that it will not externally change in any way in the course of its journey. But when it enters the door it is aiming for, then something changes. The receiver of the message — poetry, preaching, music, architecture, painting — says, 'Now this is part of me. It is mine.' A change takes place in him, but it also takes place in *it*. How would this better be described than by saying that its accidents remained unaltered, but its substance had changed? The dry formula communicates nothing of the 'explosion' we are celebrating; but when we speak of the Elements of the Communion being the Body and Blood of Christ we mean that they make Christ part of us: they make him ours. 'When he is mine and I am his, what can I lack or need?' Thus we sing, and that is what we mean. It is of no interest to anyone what objectively happens to the Elements while they are still in the bottle or the box, before they are consecrated. The question is whether it can ever be explained what makes them Him to us. Of course, it cannot be explained — but at least there is an area of human experience, which is the only area in which one person is real to another, in which what the coiners of dogma were trying to explain is equally explicable, and equally a mystery.

For all these reasons I hold that it is impossible for worshipers to receive what the Eucharistic Liturgy waits to communicate unless they are trained in all this area of communication. That must not be taken to mean that I hope somebody will open a School of Communication Training whose graduates alone should be admitted to the altar. As Paul would say, 'God forbid' (by which he not seldom means, 'Kindly don't attribute such nonsense to me.'). What I want here to liberate is something which is imprisoned by civilization much oftener than by ignorance, and never by innocence. People who in my own experience have 'had difficulty' with the Communion have been puritan Christians of a thoughtful mind and responsible attitude. The last English church I ministered in was served — though before my own time — by several elders who would not attend Communion. [342]

Such people had, in my view, been robbed of their faith, in this field, by custom and tradition. It is, as we have before said, one of the great blessings of our age that the Eucharist is being brought back to its proper place as the center of Christian worship in so many Christian denominations. But by itself liturgical prescriptions will not be enough to undo the damage that has been done. For what happened to many people was that the Communion began to appear to be something superstitious which their intelligence could not accept. (People like Bernard Shaw didn't help when they referred to the Sacrament as 'the pagan custom of eating the god.' Describing a performance of the Bach Chaconne as drawing the tail of a horse over the guts of a cat may be funny once). This was because worship for them had become a matter of receiving propositions which they could accept or reject. Worship conditioned by the wrong sort of preaching (it must have been the wrong sort, to have this effect: not liberating but 'challenging' or 'interesting' — making people say no more than, 'We will hear thee more on this matter') was worship in which the bloom of mystery could not do anything but fade. But more than that: where the ethos of worship is merely rational it is bad enough; [343]

154

where it is irrational, it is far worse. That which is rational has its proper place in worship (process Two, § 78, you will remember). It is a case of 'this you should do, but not leave the other undone'. If then modern liturgies are not so interpreted as to enthrone reason in its proper domain, and then enthrone mystery where it is entitled to rule, Communion will become a superstition, or a social habit, or a matter of discipline, or something that just goes unnoticed.

But we have one more thing to say concerning Mystery, and it must be said now in a different context: that of the Communion of Saints.

# Epilogue
## Communion of Saints

The last question to be asked in this book must then be, 344
'What, in communication, is the relation between the *I* and the
*We?*' In liturgical thinking and precept this question has during
recent decades become prominent, although, as we said in § 298
above, it had actually been very much in the minds of liturgical
thinkers for at least a century and a half. But although in practice
we shall probably always find that a certain lack of ideal balance
informs whatever views come to the front of discussion, the theory
must be that the two forces represented in 'I' and 'We' must be so
controlled as to produce some sort of equilibrium.

The reader will probably feel that the predisposition of the 345
theses here maintained has been towards the 'I', because we have
so constantly represented communication in terms of the building
up of the immediately destructible 'I'. Well, that formula does, in
calling for the destroying or transforming of the 'I' sufficiently
dispose of any such objection provided we can say explicitly what
is to become of the 'I' when, once aroused, it has disappeared. To
be brief, and indeed obvious, it disappears into the 'We', and in
that process makes its contribution to the building up of the
Communion of Saints.

"Communion of Saints" is one of two possible translations of 346
the Latin words in the Apostles' Creed, *communio sanctorum*,
which can of course also mean the sharing of sacred things. But to
most people it does mean a community of people. Theologically,
however, saying "I believe in the communion of saints" can lead to
a notion that the 'saints' are a closed company, defined by this
pleasant sounding phrase, which is not interested in adding to its
number. Such an idea, if taken to its logical conclusion, is
obviously suicidal, since it would preclude even the possibility of
propagating their own kind; without going quite as far as that,
certain casts of puritan mind have in history combined a belief in

the continuing duty of 'saints' to be 'separate' with a marked lack of interest in adding to the earthly company of saints.

Indeed, the 'I'-'we' tension repeats itself in the 'large-group'- 347 'small group' tensions, in the church just as in society. One of the reasons why the 'I'-'we' tension is felt so strongly just now is that the ecumenical movement has aroused many conflicting loyalties between groups, and the general tendency in the earlier twentieth century has been to attribute more fruitful virtues to large groups than to small ones. Denominational loyalties, in the theology of the marketplace, have been things which grown people ought to set aside.

The tension between what we have to call ultimately the 348 Catholic and the Puritan views of the place of the church in the world is a real one, and the proper thing to do with tensions is to use them as stabilizing agents, not to complain of them and try to pretend that they are not there. One of St Paul's most profound contributions to Christian thought was his idea of the church as the 'body of Christ'; but nowhere does he encourage us to think that the purpose of God in the world is totally achieved until all humanity has become the Body of Christ. His use of that figure has the special purpose of reactivating in Christians their sense of vocation, of stimulating their sense of community. The only place where he urges Christians to separate themselves from society is when he is inviting them to take reasonable precautions against catching the infection of false or evil values. (He is often criticized in these latter days for giving so little encouragement to those who see Christian witness in terms of defying the established conventions of society.).

But contemporary Christians do not need reminding that 349 each 'I' is part of a 'we'; on the contrary, they need reminding that there will be no 'we' unless the 'I' is properly nourished, matured, and given its cross to take up. We refer back to the point we made earlier that symphonies are not written by committees; we can readily add that they need a very devoted committee to perform them; but on the principle that we enunciated at the end of the last chapter (§ 341-3) what makes its impact on each 'I' present will make it in a different and private way, liberating each separate 'I' that is receptive to its message. And there exactly is the creative tension.

The Communion of Saints is a Christian expression for a 350 society that uses this tension to support a structure. Creation begins with an I AM: it sees a Creation which is what it will be. It resigns its limitless freedom and power of choice to that Creation.

It becomes subject to it. It, the all-free, all-powerful 'I', accepts the possibility of saying 'Now, I cannot.' And the Creation lives. The 'I' has exchanged its life for the being of the creature. Let the creature rebel: the 'I' will go to the cross for it. Let the creature think it has extinguished the 'I': the 'I' lives again. The 'I' gives the Spirit which renews, transforms the life of the creature, and the creature says 'YES!'

This is the process that is going on in the Communion of 351 Saints as often as the sparks fly in an internal combustion engine. Countless microscopic Selves create energy by losing themselves in other Selves. When the process falters a deposit of death begins to form. Where there should be life, sparking across from this Self to that, there is only something black and dim and lifeless. Coked up though the engine is, it still fires. Baxter put it like this:

> He wants not friends that hath thy love,
> and may converse and walk with thee,
> and with thy saints, here and above,
> with whom for ever I must be.

> In the communion of saints
> is wisdom, safety, and delight;
> and when my heart declines and faints
> it's raised by their heat and light.

Heat and light! Energy — that is what communication generates. The energy of the personal 'YES!' building up the continuum of the Communion of Saints.

> As for my friends, they are not lost,
> the several vessels of thy fleet,
> though parted now, by tempests toss'd,
> shall safely in the haven meet.

"Though parted now": parted indeed we are — party against party, denomination against denomination, interest against interest. 'Lack of communication' is every striker's complaint, every discontented subordinate's grievance.

St. Paul, wrestling with the most grievous of his difficulties — 352 how to persuade his own people (as he had been persuaded) of the reality of Christ, burst out: "But how are men to call on him in whom they have not believed? And how are they to believe in him of whom they have never heard? And how are they to hear without a preacher? And how can men preach unless they are sent?" *Sent!* Energy that inspires to create energy!

There is an old puritan doctrine of the priesthood of all 353 believers. In Christian communities of the puritan kind, each

159

member of a congregation at the Eucharist passes the Elements to his neighbor. The priesthood is the calling to be a vessel of energy — and that, they say, is there for any believer to accept and pass on. They say it rightly. The artist knew it all the time. For just as the preacher says, "Would that all the Lord's people are prophets" — and the New Testament tells him that they all can be — so the artist's prayer that "all the Lord's people might be artists" is answered in the promises of Pentecost.

The Communion of Saints is an idea that has fallen out of   354
shape through being hung on the wrong text. For all its heraldic illuminations (which I have long differed from Luther in valuing highly) the Book of Revelation is the wrong text for this. Those endless unisonal shouts express cosmic delight in the Lamb but not the whole of what the Lamb did for the cosmos. It is Pentecost that provides the true pattern: the only world in which the I and the We are not at war with each other. 'Every one of you brings a song. . . .' in I Corinthians 14; and what is edified is the whole body, or, in Charles Williams's image, the whole City. The City is the field of duty: delight begins by being private. Duty and delight meet in the City.

Understanding begins by being private: any other City says,   355
in the end, 'Never mind whether you understand: just obey and we shall all be at least moderately happy.' Pentecost is described by saying, 'They all *understood,* in language that suggests that 'understand' for the first time has a first person plural. The Spirit, formerly reserved for the chosen, the distinguished, the unrepeatable, is now for the community. The keeping private of what cannot live except it be shared is the grief of Ananias and Sapphira: the subjection of the private, the critical, the doubting, to the consensus of the crowd controlled by the eloquence of a spiritual oppressor is the error of Simon Magus and Apollos. The City is now an 'All' in whose company each is at his best. The believer, with his intensely personal 'Abba' is a 'One', a 'Self', an 'I' who need no longer seek the All merely as an antidote to loneliness.

356

With all the powers my poor soul hath
of humble love and loyal faith
thus low, my God, I bow to thee
whom too much love bowed lower for me.

Down, down, proud sense! Discourses, die,
and all adore faith's mystery!
Faith is my skill, faith can believe
as fast as love new laws can give.*

Is there a world in which 'I do not understand' is a condition I can accept without leaving superstition to have its way with me? Is it possible ever, anywhere, to relax into the truth? If discourses die, shall I be defended against the demons? McLuhan made a great to-do about it all; but if *The Gutenberg Galaxy* protests that intellect and literacy by themselves are not a total defense against the demons, and that our present age has come to intellectual grief because it thought they were, it is right. The mystery of Faith is not an enslavement but a liberation. The Explosions crackle away and their light illuminates the pilgrim's path better than the unaided light of reason. 'Down, down, proud sense.' But why need it be so proud? The Communion of Saints is a company of listeners: if it were not it would have no hope of being a good choir.

---

*Adoro te devote,* uncertainly attributed to St. Thomas Aquinas, translated by Richard Crashaw and John Austin, 1668.

# INDEX

References are to paragraphs. Leading ideas are referred to places where they begin, or where they are resumed.